COMPUTER SCIENCE
Pure and Simple

Fun Programming for Homeschoolers
Grades 7 - 12

COMBINED EDITION

of the award-winning homeschool classics,
Computer Science Pure and Simple Books 1 and 2,
providing only the programming lessons

by Phyllis Wheeler & Don Sleeth

For use with MicroWorlds EX Logo Software

Motherboard Books

First Combined Edition

© Copyright 2015 by Motherboard Books

ISBN 978-0692431627

MicroWorlds is a trademark of Logo Computer Systems, Inc.

The use of registered names, trademarks, etc. in this publication does not imply, even in the absence of a specific statement, that such names are exempt from the relevant laws and regulations and therefore free for general use.

Table of Contents

Introduction

Computers are all around us, and the workplace clearly requires them. Many of the good jobs that will be open for our kids when they grow up will involve programming. And so homeschoolers really need to be learning computer science. They'll be learning logic at the same time, sharpening their reasoning skills.

The earlier kids start a complex subject, the better. But many home-schooling parents think they are not qualified to teach computers. In the meantime, their kids may be falling behind in acquiring a skill that they will surely need.

If you need some help teaching computer programming to your teens, this book is for you. You CAN give your kids the early training in computers that will make them comfortable directing this medium all their lives.

Computer Science Pure and Simple contains plenty of work with variables, and so is suited to students who are at least 12 years old. A variable is an abstract concept that younger children are not ready for. Younger children can take advantage of *Logo Adventures*, a MotherboardBooks.com curriculum teaching Logo programming and reasoning skills (with a strong creative flavor) to elementary-aged kids as young as 8, without the use of variables.

Computer Science Pure and Simple grew out of the efforts of a homeschool co-op in St. Louis, Missouri. It represents a transcription of our efforts to teach to computer novices.

If you don't have the MicroWorlds EX software, stop now and get it from www.MicroWorlds.com . A free trial download is available. Those who prove purchase of this book to the MicroWorlds people should receive a coupon code for 70 percent discount off retail price. Contact info@MicroWorlds.com and info@MotherboardBooks.com .

Pacing, testing

The suggested pacing for this material is one lesson per week, allowing time for exercises and practice before moving on. We figure the amount of time spent is about 3 hours per week, at one lesson per week. Thirty-four lessons will then provide 102 hours of instruction, which is one high school credit in our state.

For the homeschool teacher, computer expertise is not required. But a little experience with computers is needed, such as ability to open and save a document.

Test your student by comparing the student's project to the project requirements. If the project meets all requirements, it gets 100 percent, and so on.

Remove the answer key before you start!

Be sure you cut out the answer key before you start. Don't let your student have control over it. We suggest that you let your student puzzle over a problem for a while before handing out some hints and then finally if necessary letting him see the answer. For troubleshooting programs that don't work, look for suggestions in the text and at the troubleshooting guide in the Appendix. You can also email info@MotherboardBooks.com if you are stuck.

Why choose MicroWorlds?

This book teaches programming using MicroWorlds, an application based on the Logo computer language. It does our job admirably:

- Using graphics, it instantly shows young programmers the results of their efforts. It makes computer science fun instead of difficult.

- It introduces students to the universal elements of computer languages, including variables and logic. Once students learn one computer language, it will be easy to pick up another.

- Simple animations are easy to make.

- Visual Basic and its variation Small Basic also provide a graphic result to programming. But I believe they were not designed with the inherent sense of fun that lies behind Logo.

- Scratch, also from MIT, is an option for younger children that is easy to use. But it doesn't contain the full capabilities of a workplace computer language in the way that Logo does. I was unable to adapt my games for Scratch because Scratch couldn't handle the complex coding.

Computer requirements

MicroWorlds EX requires

PC: Windows operating systems from Window 2000 to current.

Mac: OSX 10.3.9 and higher.

The software is kept current with operating system releases.

About the Authors

Phyllis Wheeler is a mechanical engineer and homeschooling veteran who taught computer science in a homeschool co-op in St. Louis. Along the way she has written some computer programs and taken some computer courses. She has also worked as a newspaper reporter and free-lance writer. She has bachelor's degrees in English from Smith College and in mechanical engineering from Washington University in St. Louis.

Don Sleeth is a computer professional in Canada.

Part 1: Introduction to MicroWorlds Programming

Using MicroWorlds EX

You should first look at tutorial videos online for MicroWorlds EX. Find them at the **support** page of www.MotherboardBooks.com.

The Procedures "Page" or window is to the right alongside the Graphics "Page," provided the Procedures tab beneath it is selected. The Command Center is to the bottom left.

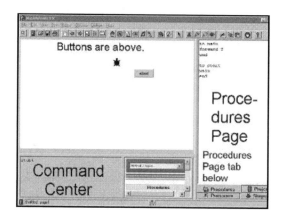

You access the Shapes Center by clicking on the **Shapes** tab below the Procedures Page section. You will need to import shapes from the drawing/painting window to your Shapes Center before using any non-turtle shapes.

Click on the icon at the top that looks like a yellow pad with paintbrush. The drawing/painting/clipart window opens up. Click on the daisy icon to see single shapes or the two-people icon to see animation shapes.

Now drag the drawing window over to the left by clicking down on the blue band at the top and holding the mouse button down, dragging sideways. Make sure the window on the right is the shape center by clicking on the tab beneath it that says **Shapes**.

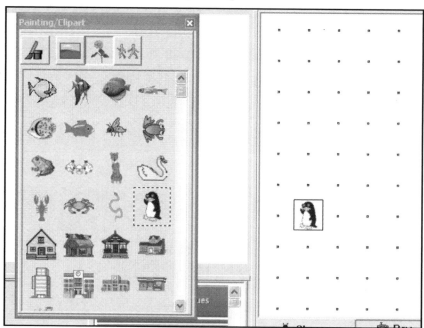

Drag individual shapes from the drawing/painting window to the Shape Center to install them, as shown above. When the shape is installed, pause your mouse over it to see its name, number, and size in pixels. Once a shape is installed in this way, you can use it in your programs.

#1 Logo Procedures and Input

What will I learn?

Logo is a programming language. To learn it we will use MicroWorlds, a computer application that you purchase separately from MicroWorlds.com. The Logo lessons in this book are intended to teach individual students in grades 5-12 the basics of computer use and programming. We will teach you some basic computer skills. We will also teach you how and why to write programs that will work properly and can be improved on as time goes by. This will give you a solid foundation in programming techniques so you can develop programs in any language.

What computer language?

There are many different programming languages, just like there are many human languages. Human languages all have verbs, nouns and adjectives. Programming languages too have similar elements, like procedures and variables. It is these building blocks that are basic to computer programming in any language that it is important to learn. Once you learn one computer language, it is much easier to learn the next and the next.

I chose Logo because it allows me to teach you to build programs that are fun and complete in a short time.

Just like human languages can be spoken with different accents, so it is with computer languages. The version of Logo that I use in these lessons is from a commercial product named MicroWorlds from Logo Computer Systems Inc.

Where are we headed?

We will learn techniques that will allow you to draw your own interesting scenes and add lots of movement and animation. Later in the book we will make several games.

What is a program?

A program is *a list of instructions to the computer*. Let's suppose we are going to give someone a list of simple instructions in English on how to set the table. This list of instructions might look like this:

> **get a plate from the cupboard**
> **walk to the table**
> **put it on the table**
> **return to the cupboard**
> **get a glass**
> **... and so on.**

But a set of instructions for a computer is written using a specific list of words that the computer can understand. For example, **forward 50** means go forward 50 turtle paces. These action words for the computer are *procedures*.

What's a turtle, you ask? It's our little drawing partner on the screen. We pretend that it is carrying a pen that it can put down, to draw, and pick up, to move around without drawing. It can wear various suits of clothes—it can look like a horse, a dog, even a house or a pond. The nice thing about it is that it obeys our every command, so long as we use words it can understand.

So, if a program is a list of instructions to the computer and an instruction is a list of procedures and MicroWorlds already knows piles of procedures, we must be ready to write a program!

Instructions and procedures

We need to begin by locating our turtle. With MicroWorlds EX, first we choose "free mode." When the drawing screen appears, we have to hatch a turtle by clicking on the hatching icon at the top . Then click on the screen, and you have a turtle.

Now, let's start with an instruction.

In the Command Center (the area at the bottom of the screen), type this:

> **pd forward 50**

Pd is for pen down. We are telling the turtle to put its pen down and move forward 50 turtle steps. Now we press **<enter>**.

The turtle obeyed us! It went 50 turtle steps forward—in the direction it was facing. We need to learn a new word, *input*. This is the number 50 in this case. The input is the number that the procedure **forward** needs to have. (Some procedures also have *outputs*: they give *you* a number.)

In the Command Center, type the following line:

> **pd forward 50 right 90 forward 50 right 90 forward 50 right 90 forward 50 right 90**

When the cursor is at the very end, press **<enter>**. Presto! Our first instruction causes the turtle to draw a square.

Let's analyze our one long line of instruction. All the words you see on the line are names of procedures:

> **pd:** a procedure that puts the current turtle's pen down and requires no inputs and has no outputs

> **forward:** a procedure that moves the current turtle in the direction its head is pointing by a certain number of steps. The number is a required input.

> **right:** a procedure that turns the current turtle to the right by a number of degrees. The number is a required input.

The last two procedures require a number as their input. One very important thing to notice is that some procedures require inputs and some don't.

Procedure inputs and output

Logo procedures can be thought of as jigsaw puzzle pieces. Our job as programmers is to build puzzles which fit together properly. The procedures that we will build, and the built-in procedures that come with MicroWorlds, have a specified number of inputs. It can be zero inputs (such as **pd**) or one input (such as **forward**) or more. A procedure can also have zero *outputs* (such as **forward**) or one output (such as **sum**).

A procedure that needs no inputs is simply a square jigsaw puzzle piece. One that needs one input has a hole on the right for a tab. The output puzzle piece next to it has a tab sticking out on the left. So they fit together. When we use procedures in an instruction we must provide the required inputs and we must provide a place for the outputs to go, in order for the whole instruction to be correct. Think of it as a one-line jigsaw puzzle.

Here is a procedure with one input:

As you can see, **forward** has a hole that needs a number input.

Procedures that expect one number as their input will have the right size opening to fit a number. The starting edge of a line of instruction must be solid, that is no output sticking out, and so must the ending edge.

Here are some instructions. Try to guess which ones will work and which ones won't.

Type them into the Command Center to test your guess.

Instruction 1

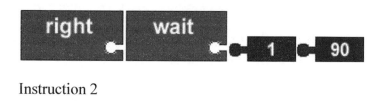

Instruction 2

Instruction 3

Instruction 4

It's really pretty easy to get the inputs and outputs all lined up and in the right order once you pretend the procedures are jigsaw pieces and the instruction must be a completed puzzle!

If an instruction is going to work, then all the openings and tabs must be used. Note that this means that an instruction can't begin with an output.

Programming with style

A computer program has to achieve more than just doing the job. It needs to have staying power—meaning that it needs to be easily understood and changed by others. Here are some goals to keep in mind when writing a program:

1. Set up the plan of attack ahead of time.
2. Use small, one-purpose-only procedures whenever possible. This makes it easy for someone to change the program later.
3. Document your work so the next person can understand it.
4. The code must work every time for everyone.
5. Choose consistent, sensible names for procedures.

Where to write your program?

First, let's talk about where *not* to write your program. If you right-click on a turtle or follow the tutorials supplied with MicroWorlds EX, you find a dialog box or "backpack" which allows you to enter your instructions for the turtle. This is NOT a good idea! Goal number 2 above says that the program must be easily read. How can it be easily read if instructions are scattered all over the place with individual turtles? The dialog boxes that are associated with the controls such as turtles and buttons are not where you want to hide your beautifully crafted code.

What you want is the Procedures Page. How do you find it?

The Procedures Page or window is to the right alongside the Graphics Page, provided the Procedures tab beneath it is selected. The Command Center is to the bottom left.

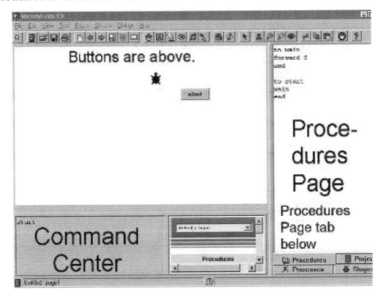

Write a procedure

Okay, remember we have an instruction that makes the turtle draw a box. Here it is again:

> pd forward 50 right 90 forward 50 right 90 forward 50 right 90 forward 50 right 90

Our beginning project is to develop procedures that make the turtle move in a variety of ways. If we left off the instruction **pd** (pen down), then we would have an instruction to make the turtle move in a square. Let's make that our first procedure.

You can teach MicroWorlds new words by writing procedures. Remember our instructions for setting the table? Let's write a "procedure" for that.

> **To SetTheTable**
> **get a plate from the cupboard**
> **walk to the table**
> **put it on the table**
> **return to the cupboard**
> **get a glass**
> **... and so on**
> **end**

Notice the procedure begins with **to** and finishes with **end**. Also, its name, SetTheTable, has no spaces. These are Logo language requirements. In this "procedure," you are giving the person you are teaching a list of instructions using words that she knows. You are, in a way, teaching her a new phrase, "set the table."

Now we are going to write a set of detailed instructions for MicroWorlds to draw a square. This is the essence of programming, namely adding new procedures and capabilities to the existing ones that came with the language.

What shall we call our new procedure? How about **square**. Then, when we want the turtle to move in the shape of a square, we can just type **square** in the Command Center, instead of that long instruction we developed above.

On the Procedures Page, type the following:

> **to square**
> **   pd forward 50 right 90 forward 50 right 90 forward 50 right 90 forward 50 right 90**
> **end**

All procedures start with the word **to** and end with the word **end.** A procedure like this adds a new word to MicroWorlds vocabulary. It uses **pd**, which puts the turtle's "pen" down, **forward 50,** which moves the turtle 50 "steps" in the direction it is facing, and **right 90,** which turns the turtle to the right by 90 degrees, or a right turn. Let's try it out! Move over to the Graphics Page. Hatch a turtle and put it on the Graphics Page. In the Command Center, type **cc** to clear the command center and push <Enter> if you need to clean out old messages. Then type **square** and press <Enter>.

Hmm, my **square** didn't work very well. I think the problem is that the turtle went so fast, you couldn't see it.

It is very common that things don't work quite right the first time. This is not a failure, it just means we can tweak our procedure to make it better!

Before we slow the movement down, there is another problem with our **square** procedure. As it is now, it is not really very readable. Let's write the same long instruction over several lines, making it much more readable. We can do that on the Procedure Page. It's just not as easy in the Command Center. MicroWorlds Logo just ignores the fact that the instruction is spread over many lines. MicroWorlds Logo is really just interested in whether the inputs and outputs are all satisfied.

Change your procedure so it looks like this:

> **to square**
>   **pd**
>   **forward 50 right 90**
>   **forward 50 right 90**
>   **forward 50 right 90**
>   **forward 50 right 90**
> **end**

There, that is much more readable and you can see at a glance how it works. Notice that our procedure **square** takes no inputs and has no output, so its puzzle piece looks like this:

It is a "satisfied" instruction all by itself.

Now back to improving our first procedure. To slow the movement of the turtle, let's add a built-in procedure, **wait**, after each turn that the turtle makes. **Wait** takes one input, a number. Change your procedure so it looks like this:

> **to square**
>   **pd**
>   **forward 50 right 90 wait 1**
>   **forward 50 right 90 wait 1**
>   **forward 50 right 90 wait 1**
>   **forward 50 right 90 wait 1**
> **end**

Go to the Graphics Page and we'll give it a try! We type **square** in the Command Center.

Does it work? Here are some general troubleshooting hints: be sure each procedure begins with **to** and ends with **end**. Make sure what you typed exactly matches what we are telling you to type.

Hey, that's much better. On the last line of the **square** procedure, you see that **wait 1** is there, even though the movement of the turtle is finished. We could remove this last **wait 1** but there is little to gain, and later we may want to use this procedure to make the turtle move round and round the square many times. In that case having the **wait 1** will make the movement even.

Let's add a comment to let any future readers know what this procedure does **(Goal 3)**. We'll make a second line like this: **;draws a square of 50 units**

```
to square
  ;draws a square of 50 units
  pd
  forward 50 right 90 wait 1
  forward 50 right 90 wait 1
  forward 50 right 90 wait 1
  forward 50 right 90 wait 1
end
```

The semicolon at the beginning of the line tells the computer not to try to read that line. So this is how we write comments to others, to say what is going on, and comments to ourselves, so that later on we will easily remember what we did.

Now we have a procedure to be proud of, but we still don't have a program.

So that you can continue with this project at another time, please save your work as **Starter.** Put it in the folder called My Documents, or make a new folder for your work.

Show your teacher that you have saved your work and that it draws a square.

Assignment 1: Write a set of instructions with at least eight lines to describe all the steps, in order, for doing a chore that you do regularly.

#2 A Simple Logo Program

Load in your work

From the file menu, open your project named **Starter.** We will make some changes to this file, and we want to keep an unchanged version. So we need a copy. From the **File** menu select **Save Project As** and save your project with a different name, say **Square**.

Let's talk for a minute about what is going on when you save a file. The computer filing system is like a filing cabinet, in a way. Think of a file as being like a piece of paper with writing on it. You can save a number of these files in a "folder." Think of a "folder" as being like a manila folder. You can put many manila folders in another manila folder.

There are big file drawers, which hold all the folders and folders inside of folders. One is called C: This is your hard drive, which remains permanently inside your computer. This is probably your biggest storage area, with a folder for each user that contains a folder called My Documents or Documents. You may have a portable flash drive; this would be E: F: or G: And there is the D: drive, your CD-ROM drive.

While we're talking about it, there's the computer "desktop." This is supposed to pretend to be your real desk, with file folders sitting out on it ready for you to pick up and work with.

In your copy of the file called Square, find your Procedures page. It should look like this:

```
to square
   ;draws a square of 50 units
   pd
   forward 50 right 90 wait 1
   forward 50 right 90 wait 1
   forward 50 right 90 wait 1
   forward 50 right 90 wait 1
end
```

Making a simple program

The Command Center makes a perfect place to test instructions and procedures. But it is not a very user-friendly place from which to launch a program. Also, later when we make stand-alone programs to run on a Web page, the Command Center doesn't show. So we need to learn to do without it.

Our Graphics Page is the page where the turtle draws squares for us. We need a clickable button right on our Graphics Page. Remember how to get there? In MicroWorlds EX, the Graphics Page is right in front of us all the time, upper left. To make the button, click the button icon and then click on the Graphics Page where you want the button to be. A dialog box pops up. Looking at it you can see that we are allowed to type in an instruction to be run when someone clicks on the button.

We want to wire this button so it starts our program.

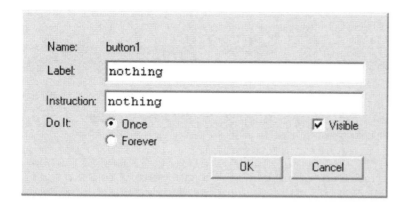

In MicroWorlds EX, we can give the button a label and an instruction. As a rule, let's make these the same thing. Put Start in both places, where it says "nothing" in the picture above.

Click OK. Then drag the button so it fits nice and tight in the bottom left corner of the Graphics Page.

I suggest you save your work often. On a PC, if you press the two keys **Ctrl** and **S** together, it will save the revised project under the name you just gave, **Square.**

Now click on the **Start** button. We get the error message "I don't know how to Start." This is exactly what we are going to teach MicroWorlds now! How are we going to teach it? You guessed it, we will create a procedure called **Start**.

Go back to the Procedures Page. Remember how? Now, to add the word **Start** to MicroWorlds' vocabulary, we need to make a **Start** procedure.

First I would like to comment on program design. Remember these lessons are to teach you good programming techniques. They are not just to teach you about MicroWorlds or Logo. The computer language C is a favorite professional language, and so is C++. Both of these languages, in particular C++, have been designed to help programmers manage the complexity of computer programs. Both of these languages start every program's execution at a procedure named **Main**. This means that the first procedure to run is always called **Main**. If you are reading a program in C or C++, you would typically start by looking for the procedure named **Main**. I feel it is a very good convention to follow.

So we will make a **Start** procedure which will call (run) our **Main** procedure. Add these to your procedures page:

> **to Start**
>   **Main**
> **end**
>
> **to Main**
>   **cc**
>   **talkto "t1**
>   **;works with turtle named t1**
>   **repeat 20 [Square]**
> **end**

Notice our new instruction, **talkto "t1**. This makes sure we are addressing the first turtle, t1, and not some other turtle. Save your work by striking **<ctrl>** and **s**.

We now have a complete program! **Main** tells the computer what to do first, then next, and so on. The procedures listed after Main tell the computer how to do the commands it doesn't know already.

The first instruction in **Main** tells MicroWorlds to clear the Command Center. This is so we know that any error messages we see are new ones. The next instruction in **Main** tells MicroWorlds which turtle should perform the actions in the following instructions. It is not necessary to have that instruction if there is only one turtle, but it improves the readability of our program, which is one of our goals.

The third line uses the built-in procedure **repeat** which requires two inputs: a number indicating how many repetitions, and a list of instructions to repeat. We only have one instruction, *so to make it into a list you just put square brackets around it.* We will be talking more about lists later.

Try running your program by going to the Graphics Page and clicking your **Start** button. Now try running it in Presentation Mode by going to the **View** menu and clicking on **Presentation Mode.** Then click the Start button. To get out of Presentation Mode, double-click on the black border.

One final bit of house cleaning to do. As this and other programs grow, your Procedures Page gets very large. So you don't waste time looking for procedures, you should keep them in alphabetical order. To move procedures around, highlight the whole procedure by putting the mouse button down above it, holding it down, and moving the cursor to the other side. Now go to the **Edit** menu, and select **cut**. The lines seem to vanish. Really you have put them on an invisible clipboard. Now move the cursor where you want the lines to be, and from the **Edit** menu select **paste**. Presto, the lines show up in the new spot! This **cut and paste** routine works in nearly all computer applications. You can also use **copy and paste** if you want to make copies.

I usually do something special with **Main** to make it particularly easy to find, such as type double lines before and after it. By the way, MicroWorlds is not case-sensitive, so it doesn't matter if you type capital or lower-case letters. Here is my Procedures Page:

```
========================
to Main
   cc
   talkto "t1
   ;works with turtle named t1
   repeat 20 [Square]
end
========================
to square
   ;draws a square of 50 units
   pd
   forward 50 right 90 wait 1
   forward 50 right 90 wait 1
   forward 50 right 90 wait 1
   forward 50 right 90 wait 1
```

end

    to Start
       Main
    end

Can you figure out how to rewrite your **square** procedure using **repeat**? Remember **repeat** needs two inputs, a number indicating how many repetitions, and a list of instructions to repeat—with brackets around it [like this].

So that you can continue with this project at another time, please save your work under its current name, **Square,** by striking **<ctrl>** and **s**. *Run* your program (by clicking on the Start button) for a teacher, and *show* you have proper format on the Procedures Page.

An assignment: Let's play with it.

- Repeat the instruction in **square** three rather than four times. Press **Start** repeatedly. What happens?
- Make larger squares.
- Wait longer.
- Try a different angle and see what you draw. This means change the input to **right**. For example, **right 34** instead of **right 90**.

(After you make these changes, save it under a different name, such as **mysquare)**. We will be pulling up **Square** later and want it to be a clean copy.)

#3: Introduction to Animations

Let's review the Shape Center.

First, we find the Drawing Center. Locate the paintbrush icon at the top 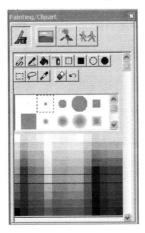. Click on it.

Look at the icons at the top:

The landscape picture allows us to choose a background. The flower icon window contains shapes, and the walking-people icon window contains shapes just for animations. Click on the walking-people animations icon.

These are shapes for the turtle to "wear." But first we have to install them into the Shape Center. Click on the blue band at the top of this shape window, and hold it down. Move the window to the left. Now, at the bottom of the page on the right, find the folder tab that says "shapes." Click on that so it's the folder that shows. It should look like a grid of dots.

Make sure your window full of possible shapes is next to the Shape Center full of empty dots.

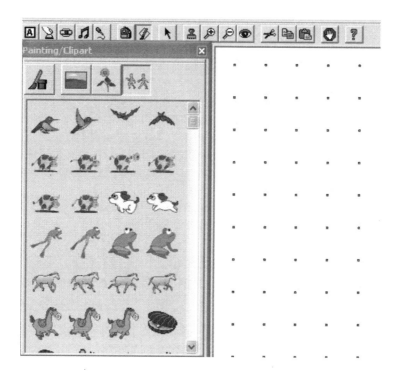

Now, let's drag some shapes over from the Painting/Clipart window on the left to the Shape Center on the right. After we install shapes like this, they have a name and number and are usable as "clothes" by the turtle.

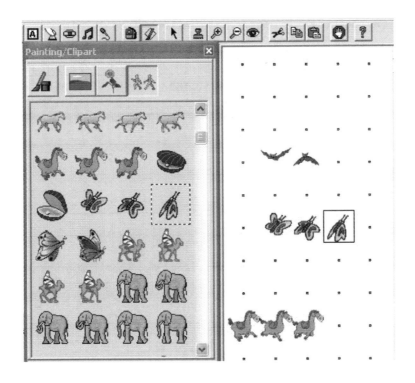

Pause your mouse arrow over one of the installed shapes, and you will see its name, number, and size in pixels. We can get rid of the Painting/Clipart window by clicking on the red x in the upper right.

Click on one of the shapes in the Shape Center, and then click on the turtle. Presto! it's wearing the shape.

You can hatch more turtles, click a shape, and click the turtle. Make the shape smaller or larger by clicking first on the magnifier icon and then on the shape. Drag the turtles around.

Getting Started

Open a new file. For now we will use **horse1, horse2,** and **horse3**. Go ahead and install your horse shapes to the Shape Center, and hatch a turtle.

We'll use the command **setsh**, for set shape. We give the computer a set list of shapes. Every time the computer calls **forward**, the computer comes back to the shapes list and tells the turtle to change shapes to the next shape. Let's set our shapes. Type this in the Command Center:

setsh [horse1 horse2 horse3]

Press **<enter>**. We're ready to go! Now let's get our turtle started walking.

23

Type this into the Command Center: **fd 1** . Execute it by pressing **<enter>** at the end of the line. What happens? The turtle takes one step, and his shape changes! Now move the cursor back up the end of that line again and press **<enter>** again to execute it. Do it again and again. Each time he changes shape! Of course this is too slow for a real animation. To really animate, the turtle needs to repeat a lot of times moving forward in small steps. We also need to add a **wait** command to pause the action enough so we can see it happening. Let's add a line:

> *setsh [horse1 horse2 horse3]*
> *pu repeat 100 [fd 3 wait 1]*

This is how an animation works: *first set your shapes, then move forward.*

At the end of the second line, push **<enter>** and see what happens. Hmm. The turtle wearing a horse shape is going upward! That's not entirely what we had in mind. Here's why: the turtle's head is still pointed up, although the shape it is wearing makes it seem like the turtle's head must be pointed to the right. The turtle always goes in whatever direction its head is pointed in. But the head is hidden if the turtle wears a shape. To see where the head is, type this into the Command Center: **setsh 0** . That returns the shape to the original turtle shape. Take a look! Then execute the **setsh [horse1 horse2 horse3]** line in the Command Center again (by putting the cursor at the end of the line and pressing **<enter>**) to get the turtle back to the way it was.

We want to tilt the turtle's head in the direction we want him to move. That is to the right. We'd like to set the turtle's heading (using **seth**, pronounced "set-H," for set heading) so that no matter what it was doing before, it will end up facing the correct direction. Type this in the Command Center right before the other command: **seth 90** . Seth 90 turns the turtle's head always 90 degrees to the right from vertical. That's the same angle that is at the corner of a rectangle. What if we had typed **rt 90**? The result would have been the same. But what if the turtle's head had started out pointing down? Then **rt 90** would have resulted in the turtle pointed the wrong way. But **seth 90** will always point the turtle to the right. We'll use **seth 90** in this case. So now our Command Center looks like this:

> *setsh [horse1 horse2 horse3]*
> *seth 90 pu repeat 100 [fd 3 wait 1]*

We don't have to keep executing the **setsh** line, unless we want to switch to a different list of shapes.

So, now we can use this code to make ourselves a procedure called **walk.** Copy and paste the two lines of code over to the Procedures Page (remember how to find it?). Now start the procedure with **to walk** and end it with **end.** Go back to the Command Center and clear it (use **cc** for Clear Command Center). Now type **walk** in the Command Center. Does the turtle walk?

OK, let's make another procedure that is a copy of **walk**, only faster. We'll call it **runn.** (I discovered that **run** is already used by the Logo language for something else, so we'll just change the spelling.) First we want to highlight and copy the procedure **walk** (use **edit-copy**) and paste (use **edit-paste**) another version below our original procedure on the Procedures Page. We'll give it the new name **runn** and make sure it ends with **end.** So the Procedures Page looks like this:

24

```
to walk
setsh [horse1 horse2 horse3]
seth 90 repeat 100 [fd 3 wait 1]
end

to runn
setsh [horse1 horse2 horse3]
seth 90 repeat 100 [fd 3 wait 1]
end
```

But of course the code for each one is the same! Let's change the code in the second one to speed up the action. I am going to let you experiment to see how to speed it up. You have two numbers to change: the input to **fd** and the input to **wait**. Type **runn** in the Command Center. Does it move faster? Change the numbers again. Go ahead and experiment! Save your work.

Now let's see if we remember how to animate. We are going to open up a new empty file and start over. Don't panic! I'll tell you how to do this. And, if you get stuck, just look at the early part of this lesson!

Remember! *First set your shapes, then move forward.* In the Shape Center, set up or locate these

shapes: **doggy1** and **doggy2** .

First set your shapes: we'll need a line like **setsh [dog1 dog2]** .

Now, what direction should the turtle face? The same way that the shape dog1 is facing. **Seth 90** faces the turtle to the right; **seth -90** faces him to the left.

Then move forward. Make him move forward slowly, using these commands: **repeat**, **fd**, and **wait**. After you have a procedure for slow movement, make one for fast movement.

Next, doctor some shapes. First we will practice. In the Shape Center, double-click on a shape to open it. This is also how you create a new shape—by double-clicking on a blank in the shape center.

The shape may take up a lot of the page. If this is the case, in the upper left corner of the page,

25

find a box that says "1100%," or some similar large number. Change that to 400 per cent by clicking on the down arrow next to the number and choosing a new one.

You notice you have drawing tools at your disposal.

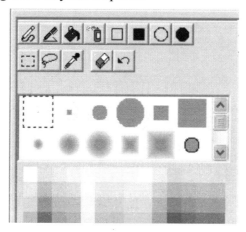

MicroWorlds EX drawing tools

You can spray paint different colors. Just choose a color, click the spray can, and click on the picture to spray. You can put solid-colored squares and circles wherever you like. Just click on the square or circle tool, then click on the screen. Try dragging with the mouse button down. You can use the paint can to fill an area that is all one color. You can use the spray-paint can to spread colored dots. You can reverse the drawing or swivel it using icons that look like these: ▓▓▓▓ ¢ 45 ▼ ↶. You can paint it with shaded squares and circles, and fill with plaids. If you want, you can save the shape. Or you can click "cancel."

So here's your next challenge: create your own three shapes for an animation. It can be an explosion (use the spray can), a simple animal made of rectangles and circles, or whatever. Since an animation consists of related shapes, it would be easiest to make something that grows rather than walks. (For a walking shape, you have to draw legs in different positions.) For a growing animation, one shape would be tiny, another medium, another large. An explosion is a growing animation.

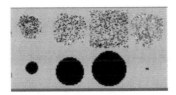

Animation Shapes by a Student

After you have created a shape, you'll notice a blank line beneath it where you can type in a name for it, for example **pow1, pow2**, or **pow3**. A name isn't necessary, though. After you save it, pause your mouse arrow over it to see how it is numbered. You can use either a name or a number to refer to it in the command **setsh**.

So you could say

> **setsh [pow1 pow2 pow3]**

or you could say

> **setsh [35 36 37]**

If your animation walks, set its heading so it moves to the side, and make it move forward by medium steps, like this:

> **seth 90 repeat 100 [fd 3 wait 1]**

If your animation grows, make it move forward by very tiny steps, one-hundredth of a step, written .01:

> **seth 90 repeat 100 [fd .01 wait 1]**

Remember, in an animation, *first set your shapes, then move forward*.

Explosion Shapes by a Student

#4 Logo Running Horse

From the file menu, open your project named **Square**. Then from the file menu select "Save Project As" and save your project as **Square1.** We are going to make some changes to this copy.

In the Procedures Page, make sure your program looks like this:

```
=====================
to Main
   cc
   talkto "t1
   ;works with turtle named t1
   repeat 20 [square]
end
=====================


to square
   ;draws a square of 50 units
   pd
   repeat 4 [forward 50 right 90 wait 1]
end

to Start
   Main
end
```

Play with your creation

Go to the Shape Center. Install some shapes.

In your Shape Center, click on a shape. Then click on the turtle on the Graphics Page. Now he is wearing the shape! Click on the Start Button. There he goes! It doesn't matter what shape the turtle is wearing. He still goes around and around in a square. Notice again that although the black turtle shape's head rotates with the direction it is traveling, the other shapes it can wear do not. So to see which way the underlying turtle is facing, you can change it back to a turtle shape.

Adjust the amount the turtle moves forward in the procedure **square.** Change the size of the turtle shape with the magnifying glass.

Let's animate the turtle. **Setsh** requires an input which is either a word (must be the name of a shape) or a list of words (must be a list of names of shapes). Here is an example of both:

```
setsh "horse1
setsh [horse1 horse2 horse3]
```

Install the **horse1, horse2,** and **horse3** shapes into your Shape Center.

In my code, why do I need to put the quotation mark in front of **"horse1**? Why not just **setsh horse1**?

When you give MicroWorlds Logo a word, like **start** or **main** or **setsh or horse1**, it assumes the word is a procedure to look up in its vocabulary and run. It treats it as an action word, or a verb. Putting the quotes in front says, "This is a name of something; don't try to run it." It says it's a noun.

So without the quotes in front of **horse1**, MicroWorlds will try to run the procedure **horse1**. But naturally, there isn't one.

Make sure the " is made by one stroke of the key next to the semicolon key, while holding down the shift key. Two strokes of the ' key won't do.

Setsh needs either a word or a list of words as its input. So, **setsh "horse1** is a complete instruction. In the second example, **setsh [horse1 horse2 horse3],** you don't have to quote each name because the brackets show that it is a list. **Setsh** will accept as its input a list of names of shapes. Therefore MicroWorlds knows to interpret the words as a list of shape names.

Change your **Main** procedure to look like this:

```
to Main
  cc
  pu
  talkto "t1
  ;works with turtle named t1
  setsh [horse1 horse2 horse3]
  repeat 20 [square]
end
```

We are using another tool: pen up, or **pu**.

Click your **Start** button. The horse is running around an invisible square! (See troubleshooting suggestions in the Appendix if you need to.)

Exercises:

*Turn your turtle turn into a running dog using **doggy1** and **doggy2**.*

Make the horse or dog run in a straight line, not a square. (Don't change the **square** procedure; just don't call it. Replace the line in **Main** that calls it with another command. What will that be? Experiment!) If he is drawing a line, have him pick his pen up.

*Increase the wait time after the **forward** command, to slow the animation down.*

Is your horse or dog floating upward? Running backward? Let's make sure the underlying turtle is facing the same direction as the horse or dog shape. In **Main**, change the direction the turtle is moving using **seth**. Remember that **seth** has a number input, for example **seth 0** . The number is a number of degrees, a measure of how much the horse-turtle is turning. **Seth 0** points the turtle's head upward. **Seth 90** points its head to the right. **Seth –90** (or **seth 270**) points it to the left. **Seth 180** points it down.

You can also flip the horse or dog shape to face the other way by double clicking on its shape in the Shape Center and then clicking the "flip" icon .

Finish your work

Hit **control-s** to save your work under the name you had given it. ***Show*** your teacher that the horse or dog runs in a straight line, not too fast, without drawing a line. Make sure that on the Procedures Page, the **Main** procedure comes first and is set off by double lines, and that the other procedures are in alphabetical order.

#5 Simple Logo House

Let's work on drawing using Logo. Open up **Square** (not Square1 from last time). **Square** should look like this:

```
========================
to Main
    cc
    talkto "t1
    ;works with turtle named t1
    repeat 20 [Square]
end
========================


to square
    ;draws a square of 50 units
    pd
    repeat 4 [forward 50 right 90 wait 1]
end

to Start
    Main
end
```

Now save it as **House**. This makes a copy of it that we will change.

So far we have only been drawing a square or a line. Let's do some experimenting to see if we can draw a triangle. Go to the Command Center and type **cc <enter>**, to clear the command center, then **cg <enter>** to clear the graphics.

First, let's talk about degrees. Degrees measure how much you are turning. When the turtle draws a square, it makes 90-degree turns. So a 90-degree turn is the measure of a right angle. But how much is a degree, anyway? In the Command Center, let's tell our turtle to put its pen down, turn one degree, go forward 50 and back 50.

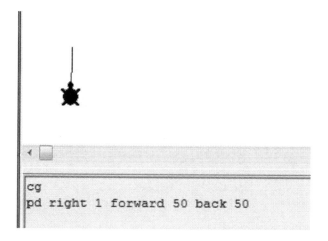

```
cg
pd right 1 forward 50 back 50
```

Hmm. How much did it turn? It's hard to tell. Obviously one degree isn't much. Now, what if we tell it to repeat those same commands 45 times?

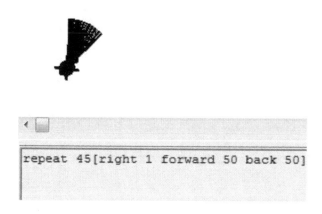

```
repeat 45[right 1 forward 50 back 50]
```

Ninety times? Enough times to go full circle? Experiment until your turtle is drawing a starburst. Remember **repeat** has two inputs: a number of times to repeat, and a list of commands to repeat. You have just learned that there are 360 degrees in a circle, and each degree is a tiny turn for the turtle.

Now, about going through the turns to draw a figure. Let's suppose YOU are a turtle, and the floor of the room you are in is the screen. If you are facing straight ahead and then turn yourself to face to the right, you have turned yourself 90 degrees.

Choose three endpoints for a big equal-sided triangle on the floor (for example, a chair, the door jamb, and a table leg.) Walk along one side of the triangle, and then turn yourself the required angle to get to the next side. Notice you have turned more than 90 degrees! In fact, you have turned 120 degrees. Go to the next corner. Turn 120 degrees. Walk to the next corner. Turn 120 degrees. You are now facing the same way you started, so you have turned a total of 360 degrees, or full circle. You have now done all the turns that a turtle would do if it were drawing an equal-sided, or equilateral, triangle.

Draw a triangle with a pencil on a piece of paper. Suppose that it is 50 turtle steps on a side. Write a set of instructions in English on a piece of paper that tells the turtle how far to walk and how far to turn. Then translate it to Logo. Use **repeat.** (Check this and other answers at the end of the book, but only after you have worked on the problem for a while. Also find a troubleshooting guide there.)

Get to the Procedures Page. Name our new procedure **To triangle**. Add a line of explanation, such as **;draws a triangle of 50 units.** Don't forget **pd.** Then type in your instructions. Finish with **end.**

Go back to the Graphics Page. In the Command Center, type **triangle** and hit enter. Did the turtle draw a triangle? If not, go back to the Procedures Page. Adjust the procedure till it works. Show your teacher that it works by going to the Command Center and typing **triangle** , then pressing **<enter>.**

We can draw a lot more than triangles. In the Command Center, play with turns of smaller angles. We'll see what happens with **right 60** instead of **right 120**, just for grins. Type in this:

> **cg**
> **pd**
> **repeat 8 [forward 50 right 60 wait 1]**

and press **<enter>.** What happened? Now replace **right 60** with **right 30**, then **right 20**, then **right 1**. You'll need to increase the number of repeats to get a good idea of what you are drawing. To return the turtle to its centered, heads-up position, type **cg**, then **pd.**

Remember pen up, or **pu.** Your turtle will be crawling around and drawing things. If you don't want a line to follow him, pull his pen up, move to another spot, and then put it down again (**pd**).

Now, let's work on calling our square and triangle procedures to make a simple picture of a house: a square with triangle on top.

Returning to the command center, let's type this:

> **cg**
> **square**
> **triangle**

What did the turtle draw? It doesn't look like a house. What is wrong? The triangle starts in the wrong place!

Our turtle needs to clear graphics, draw a square making right turns, pick its pen up, then move up to the roof and face along one line of the triangle before it starts drawing the roof triangle. Imagine you are the turtle, and write down instructions for yourself in English using a piece of paper. Translate them to Logo. What combination of **pu, forward,** and **right,** with inputs, will do the trick? Here's another function you may need: **seth**, pronounced set-H, for set heading. Remember that **seth 0** points the turtle up; **seth 90** points it to the right; **seth –90** points it to the left; **seth 180** points it down.

Then type your commands into the Procedures Page. To test them, go to the Command Center and type the name of the procedure.

Name this procedure **climb.to.roof,** which MicroWorlds reads as all one word, a name. Don't forget the beginning and end words, and a line of explanation.

On the Procedures Page, create another procedure called **to house** that explains what it is doing, clears graphics, and then calls the procedures **square, climb.to.roof,** and **triangle.** End it with **end.**

Save your work by striking the control and s keys, **<ctrl> <s>.** *Show* your teacher that your program draws a house when you type **house** and press **<enter>** in the Command Center.

Assignment--prepare for Skyscraper Project:

With a pencil, draw an interesting building of at least five stories with at least three different architectural elements (door, window, porch). It can have a number of windows the same size, or two doors the same size.

#6 Add to Logo House

Open **House,** and rename it as **House1.** Let's make some improvements to our house.

We'll start with a door. We'd like the door to be somewhere in the front wall of the house, which we remember starts out as a square of 50 units in length, so the house is 50 units long. Let's write ourselves some instructions in English first. Remember that the turtle is at the upper left side of the square, facing upward and toward the right along the roof line, when it has finished drawing the house. Where to now? How about if we:

> **pick the pen up**
> **face downward**
> **climb down from the roof to the ground**
> **and turn to face to the right (using seth).**

Then we can move forward say 20 units

> **put the pen down**
> **turn to face upward again**
> **and draw a door. (This will take a combination of forward and turn commands.)**

First, make a sketch of your house showing its measurements. This will help you envision how far the turtle has to go, and how much it turns.

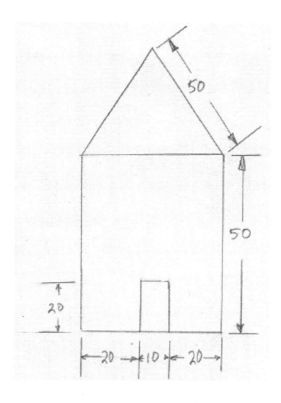

Make your list of commands in English on paper first. When you can pretend to be a turtle and follow them, it's time to translate into Logo and type them into the Command Center to see if they work. When they do, copy them and paste them onto the Procedures Page. Make procedures called **move.to.door** and **door**, and call them from **house.** When your program draws a house with a door, show your teacher. Save your work using **<ctrl> s** under the name you already gave it.

Here is what it may look like.

Now, make a window. Start with a drawing again:

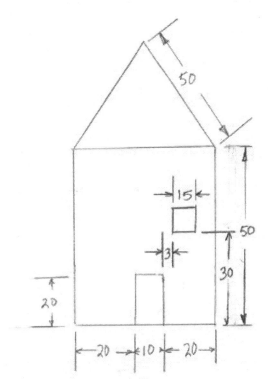

Write code that moves the turtle along the measurements that you are seeing in your drawing. Make another window and a chimney on your own. If you have time, add stairs.

Color your house using Logo instructions. Here's how you do it: you imagine that the turtle carries a bucket of paint with it. You assign the color in that bucket using **setc** (pronounced "set C" for set color) with a number input. For example **setc 15** fills the bucket with red. You can also use the name of the color as an input, if you do it with a quote mark like this:

setc "red

Find other colors by trial and error, or by using the Help menu. Right-click on a color in the painting window.

You can make a procedure called **colorhouse**. In it, pick the pen up (pu), move the turtle a few steps into the space you want to color, assign a color using **setc**, and use the built-in command **fill** to "dump the bucket." For example:

```
to colorhouse
    pu
    forward 3
    setc 15
    fill
end
```

When the house program is working properly, **show** your teacher. Save your work using **<ctrl> <s>** under the name you already gave it.

Skyscraper project assignment:

We are going to make some "code" in English to start with. Take your drawing of a big building. Put measurements on it, like we did on our house drawing. Now, make some instructions in English for drawing it. Make a Main procedure that describes how to draw the building in just a few lines in English. (For example: draw the outline, move the turtle, draw the door, move the turtle, draw a window, move the turtle ...). Then for each of those lines, make a procedure that says in detail how to follow the step in English. Remember, our goals call for procedures that have one purpose only.

#7 Logo Skyscraper Project 1

Now it is time to draw the big skyscraper!

If you have done your assignments, you have made a careful drawing of a skyscraper designed by you. You have a list of how to do it, in English. Now you need to translate to Logo.

You already have the tools you need to do this, except for the concept of a row of windows. To make a row of windows, create a procedure called **windowrow**. In it, use the **repeat** command to repeatedly draw a window plus the space between it and the next window. For instance, **window** and **windowrow** could look like this:

```
to window
  seth 0
  pd
  repeat 4 [forward 5 right 90]
end

to windowrow
  repeat 15 [pd window seth 90 pu forward 10]
end
```

Start a new file for this project. You can name it MyBuilding. Write your main procedure first. This will serve as a list of procedures that you will create, for example:

```
to Main
  cg
  movedown
  outline
  move1
  door
  move2
  windowrow
end
```

Now you need to write the first of these procedures and test it. You can do this in the Command Center, where you can watch the turtle moving as you type in commands. First create a set of commands that draws your outline. Then highlight them, **copy** them using the **edit** menu, and **paste** them on the Procedures Page. Add a procedure name, "to," and "end."

For example, your **outline** procedure in the Command Center might look like this:

```
seth 0
pd
repeat 2 [forward 150 right 90 forward 50 right 90]
pu
```

So you highlight all of them and copy them to the Procedures Page. Put "**to outline**" at the top, and "**end**" at the bottom, and you have a procedure. You can call the procedure from the Command Center by typing its name there. Remember to make procedures that do one thing (draw an outline) not two (such as move to a spot and draw an outline). Add a comment (starting with "**;**") to each procedure telling what it does. Test it by typing **outline** in the Command Center and pressing **<enter>.**

Now write the next procedure, test it, and so on. Look for chances to use the built-in procedure **repeat**, which can repeat any procedure that you write. Also, don't forget **pd** and **pu** as you move the turtle around.

As you work, remember our goals for programming with style:

1. Set up the plan of attack ahead of time.

2. Use small, one-purpose-only procedures whenever possible. This makes it easy for someone to change it later.

3. Document your work so the next person can understand it.

4. The code must work every time for every one.

5. Choose consistent, sensible names for procedures.

#8 Logo Skyscraper Project 2

Improve your building. Add at least three more items: steps, porches, and decorative columns on the corners, for example. See the troubleshooting guide in the appendix if you need to. You can color your building using programming commands such as **pu, fd 3, setc 15,** and **fill**. Add a Start button.

Skyscraper Project Requirements

Requirements:

- Your program works.

- Your building must have an outline plus at least three different features (window, door, antenna). It must also have three enhancements, such as steps, porches, or columns. Color using programming commands is extra credit. (Extra credit items are not extra for high school students.)

- Procedures do one thing (draw a window or move to another spot, but not both).

- Each procedure contains a comment, for example, **";moves up and over to the next window position."**

- **Main** is set off by double lines. Other procedures are in alphabetical order.

- For extra credit, create a program that makes an enhancement to a cityscape, such as a bridge, a newsstand, or a tree.

Make sure your project meets these requirements, and hand it in to your teacher for evaluation against the requirements.

#9 Logo Variables

Now we are going to pick up our Logo programming again. What if we want to draw a building, like before, but this time we want to be able to tell the computer to draw it twice as big? Or half as big? We will be able to do this easily once we figure out how to use *variables*. These are values, like the height of the building, that can vary, or change, but at the same time are represented with just one name. *Height* is an example of a variable name.

Let's talk variables

When you start a program, such as MicroWorlds, Word or Excel, you usually double-click on an icon. This is an instruction to the operating system to look on the hard drive and find the program that is associated with the icon. When the operating system finds it, the operating system reads it into working memory (also called loading it) and executes or 'runs' the program. This is why, in the PC world, files that run usually end with ".exe" for execute. Working memory is the place where programs are temporarily stored and where they live as they are running. This is the RAM that you buy when you buy your computer. In it there are millions of places, each with an address, where the program, and we as programmers, can store things.

Pigeonhole Mailbox Named Gus

Imagine that the working memory contains a bunch of pigeonholes, like mailboxes in a post office. To use one of these storage places, here's what we have to do: we need to reserve the spot and name it. Let's pick one and give it a name—how about "Gus?" Then we can use Gus to hold a number, word, or list. Suppose we want to use or change what's in the mailbox. Since we have named the mailbox, we can tell the computer where to find it.

So, how do we go about reserving and naming the storage spot? MicroWorlds has some built-in procedures and operators to assist us. Here is one:

Local reserves and names a storage place. Let's set up a test program to investigate using **local**.

Test program

Open MicroWorlds, and then open a new project. You can name it **Test** and save it.

Now we will make a little procedure to use to experiment with variables. We'll call our first variable Var1. We want to reserve and name our variable (storage place) using **local**.

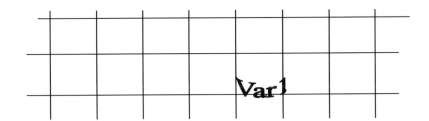

Mailbox Named Var1

Let's make a procedure called TestVar, for test variables. Type the following procedure on the Procedures Page:

> **to TestVar**
>   **local "Var1 ;reserves and names a storage place**
>   **show "Var1 ;we want to print the value in the storage place**
> **end**

Show is just a command that prints the item out in the Command Center, so we can see what the computer is thinking.

OK, so does it work? Test it by typing **TestVar** in the Command Center.

Hmm, something does print there! But what is going on?

Let's set up a Start button. Make the button, label it **Start**, and on the Procedures Page add this:

> **To Start**
>   **Main**
> **end**

Also make a **Main**:

> **To Main**
>   **TestVar**
> **end**

Go back to your Graphics Page 1 and click on the Start button. In the Command Center you will see the computer print this:

> **Var1**

Oops! This is the name of the variable (mailbox), not what is in the mailbox (a number).

The built-in procedure **local** is a procedure with one input—the name of the variable, in this case **Var1**. **Local** tells MicroWorlds to reserve a spot in memory to store things in, and it tells MicroWorlds that we will name this spot **Var1**. The spot is a little mailbox with an address of **Var1**.

As always, it helps to view the jigsaw puzzles, which show that **local** uses **Var1** for an input:

43

Now let's look at the puzzle pieces for **show**:

Show is also using **Var1** for an input. Remember that the quote mark **"** before a word tells MicroWorlds that the word we are using is the name of something, a noun, rather than the name of a procedure, which is more like an action word, or verb.

Here is the procedure we are talking about, again:

to TestVar
    local "Var1 ;reserves and names a storage place
    show "Var1 ;we want to print the value in the storage place
end

So, now we have created our variable using **local**. But we haven't stored any value in it yet. We need another procedure for that. Here it is, a bit of punctuation! **":"** allows us to grab the value that is in a variable for us to use. We read this colon as "what's in."

I want to know what the value is inside the memory spot named Var1. But the line, **show "Var1**, is an instruction to put the *word* Var1 on the Command Center. This is not really what I meant!

We will say **show :Var1,** meaning *show what's in Var1*. There is no space between the colon and the name after it.

Change your **TestVar** procedure as follows:

to TestVar
    local "Var1 ; reserves and names a storage place
    show :Var1 ; show what's in Var1
end

and run your program. Here is the result I get:

Var1 has no value in TestVar

We're getting there. We got an error message, telling us that we haven't put a value into the storage space. When we look at our procedure we can see this is true, we made a storage space (a variable) but we didn't tell MicroWorlds what to put it in it. We goofed. **It is a programming error to try to use a value from a variable if none has ever been stored there.**

So how do we put a value in the variable? We have one more procedure to learn. There is a built-in procedure **make** that does the job of storing values in previously named variables. It takes two inputs and has no outputs. The first input is the name of the variable, and the second is the value to be stored. It looks like this:

Change your procedure to the following:

to TestVar
    local "Var1 ;creates and names a variable
    make "Var1 20 ;puts the value 20 in the variable
    show :Var1 ;prints the value in the variable
end

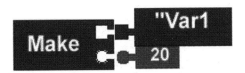

Or, using our mailbox diagram,

Mailbox With Contents

Lets take a look at what we have written in our **TestVar** procedure so far.

    We use **local** to make a variable named **Var1**

    We use **make** to put the value **20** in the variable.

    We use **show** to show **:Var1**, *the value stored in Var1.*

    I think it should all work this time! Before you run your program, so that your Command Center shows only the newest messages, add the **cc** instruction in **Main**, like this:

to Main
  cc
  TestVar
end

This of course just clears out the Command Center as you start your program each time. Now run your program.

Bingo! The value stored is **20**! Let's put in 20 and then replace it with 50, and see what happens.

```
to TestVar
   local "Var1
   make "Var1 20
   show :Var1  ; this means show the value stored in Var1
   make "Var1 50
   show :Var1
end
```

Here's what shows in my Command Center:

20
50

Again, using our mailbox diagram,

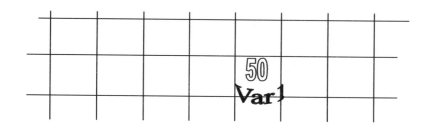

Mailbox With New Contents

We replaced the value stored, and the first one is gone forever.

What about storing a word instead of a number? Be sure to put a quote mark before the word. Try this:

```
to TestVar
   local "Var1
   make "Var1 20
   show :Var1
   make "Var1 "Me
   show :Var1
end
```

Pretty neat, eh!

46

Let's make another variable to play with.

```
to TestVar
    local "Var1
    make "Var1 20
    local "Var2
    make "Var2 50
    show :Var1
    show :Var2
end
```

What does your command center look like? It should show 20, then 50. But in this case, there are two mailboxes!

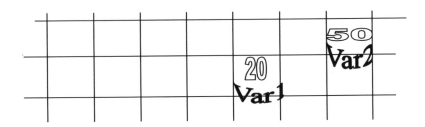

Two Mailboxes With Contents

Here is a built-in procedure that is easy to use, **sum**. It takes 2 inputs, both numbers, and has one output (the answer). If you wanted to add 2 and 3, you would write **sum 2 3**, since outputs come after the procedure name. The answer you can **show**, or store in a variable, or whatever.

Try this:

```
to TestVar
    local "Var1
    make "Var1 20
    local "Var2
    make "Var2 50
    show :Var1
    show :Var2
    show sum 20 15
    show sum :Var1 15
end
```

47

What's that last line all about? We are adding two numbers. One is the value stored in Var1, and the other is 15. Then we are printing the result. Your Command Center should say 20 50 35 35.

It is an excellent exercise to draw the jigsaw puzzle form of a line of instruction, especially before you run it. It can really help you learn what's going on. It is neat to see the way the Logo procedures all fit together with their inputs and outputs.

Try adding these lines to **TestVar**. Remember, **sum** has two inputs. Can you tell what they are doing?

> **show sum :Var1 :Var2**
> **show sum :Var1 sum 15 30**

And of course, make up your own lines to experiment with.

Talk like Logo

Another way to be sure you are understanding how a Logo instruction works is to "talk" your way through an instruction. I will do this one:

> **show sum 20 15**

I am MicroWorlds Logo. I see the procedure **show**. This procedure tells me to take one input and put it on the Command Center. I need one input.

- I see the procedure **sum**. It has an output that I can use to satisfy my need for an input. But first I need two inputs for **sum** before I can calculate the output.
- The inputs for **sum** are the two numbers 20 and 15.
- Now I know the output of **sum**, it is **35**
- So now I can satisfy the input to **show**. I will put **35** on the Command Center.

Exercise:

*Write a procedure **testSize** (instead of **testVar**) that will do the following:*

*Reserve and name a memory spot called **size**. Rewrite **Testvar**. Instead of **Var1,** create a variable called **size**.*

Store the value of five in the spot.

*Instead of **Var2**, reserve and name a variable called **height**.*

*Take your height in inches, and store it in the variable **height**.*

*Print the current value of **size**.*

*Print the current value of **height**.*

*Add 3 to the value of **size** and store the result in the same place, **size**.*

*Print the current value of **size**.*

#10 Logo Animation Using Variables

Now we will make use of our new knowledge of variables. First, type in the following. Save under a new name. It should look like this:

```
======================

to Main

end
======================


to square
    repeat 4 [forward 50 right 90 wait 1]
end

to Start
    Main
end
```

Now it's time to add an action figure. I want you to add some lines to Main so it looks like this:

```
======================

to Main
    cc
    talkto "t1
    setsh [horse1 horse2 horse3]
    repeat 20 [square]
end

======================
```

Put the **horse1, horse2**, and **horse3** shapes into your Shape Center.

Adding an input to our procedure

A while back, I suggested that it would be nice if we could decide how big a square our turtle should make. Then we would have a nice, general procedure that could be used anytime we want a square of any size. You won't believe how easy it is to make this improvement, now that we understand variables.

We want to turn our procedure **square,** which currently has no inputs and no outputs, into a procedure that receives one input. We do that simply by thinking of a good name for the input — how about length?—and putting it on the line that declares the procedure. Since we are passing the *value* in length, we will use **:length**. Make the following change to **square:**

```
to square :length
    repeat 4 [forward 50 right 90 wait 1]
end
```

We just used a shortcut! Instead of using the instruction **local,** we created the variable another way.
We put the variable name in the first line of the procedure. This also takes a spot in memory and
names it **length** so we can store a value in it.

Again, using our mailbox diagram,

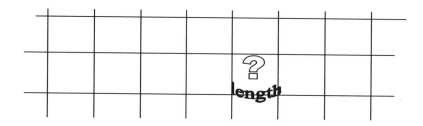

Mailbox With Unknown Contents

The neat thing is that we don't have to use **make** to put the value in. We pass the value to the
square procedure when we call it. In other words, when we use the **square** procedure in Main, we
need to place an input next to it that will go into the mailbox. The code in Main needs to say, for
example,

> **square 5**

instead of

> **square**

The 5 would go into the mailbox which is part of the procedure **square**. That mailbox is named
length.

Here's an example of a procedure we already know that needs an input: **forward**. Whenever we
type **forward**, we have to put a number after it for input. Somewhere, somebody has already
written a procedure for **forward**, which starts with **to** and has a variable name in the first line. Now
our **square** procedure will be like that, requiring a number input.

So **square** now needs one input. Its jigsaw piece looks like this:

We need to change **Main** so that when it calls **square**, it satisfies **square's** new need for an input. Let's give it the number **30**. So instead of typing **square**, we will type **square 30**.

```
to Main
    cc
    talkto "t1
    setsh [horse1 horse2 horse3]
    repeat 20 [square 30]
end
```

Now you can try your program and you will find that it works, but it really isn't any better than before. Our revised procedure square requires an input, and gets an input, but it doesn't actually use it for anything!

Let's fix **square** so that it makes use of the variable **length.** We want the value stored in **length** to be used as the input to **forward.** Do you remember how? Take a minute to think about it.

To get the value of a variable (the thing in the mailbox), use a colon before the variable name. Change your **square** procedure as follows. The change is in italics:

```
to square :length
    repeat 4
      [forward :length right 90 wait 1]
end
```

Now, to find the input for **forward,** Logo must find the value stored in **length.** Where did that value come from? The value is stored there when Main calls the procedure **square** using a number.

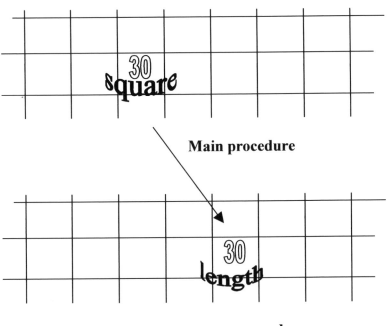

square procedure

Play with your new, more powerful **square** by changing this calling value in **Main**. Officially this value is called an "*argument*." (I don't know why. I'm not mad, are you mad?) Inside the procedure the variable is called a *parameter*.

You can also call **square** directly from the Command Center, for example by typing **square 200** and pressing **<Enter>**.

We have now finished a very good procedure that we can use any time we want. Here is my finished program:

```
==============
to Main
  cc
  talkto "t1
  setsh [horse1 horse2 horse3]
  repeat 20 [square 30]
end
==============

to square :length
  repeat 4
    [forward :length right 90 wait 1]
end

to Start
  Main
end
```

Test it! Put in different values for the line in **Main** that calls **square**. Use **square 40** and **square 60**. Look over your Procedures Page and make sure it is free of errors and nice and neat. Then save your project.

Our house size can change!

Our next task is to apply what we just learned to the house we made. We are going to add the capability to re-size the house easily. In **Main**, we are going to change the lines that call the procedures, in order to add a number input. Then when we click the Start button, **Main** will draw a house that is half as big, or twice as big. If you think about it, you will see that this variable idea is very powerful. In fact, it is a foundational idea for programming. And now you too can do it.

Go to **File Open Project** and load your house file. Rename it, using "save as," calling it "resize house."

The first thing to do is take a procedure, say **triangle**. Let's go through it and re-state all the numbers that are used for input to **forward** or **back**. You can replace each "forward" or "back" input number with a number times one. For example, **forward 50** becomes **forward 50 * 1.** (Put the ones last. This prevents silly errors later.) Note that the computer-language sign for multiplication is a star, not an x, and that there are spaces between inputs.

Do NOT replace angles, namely the inputs for **right, left**, or **seth**. The angles stay the same even if we make the house twice as big.

Now we are going to replace all those ones with a variable (a spot that holds a value). Let's call the variable **trisize**. To create and name the variable, we will add an argument to the first line of our triangle procedure, like this:

to triangle :trisize

Again, using our mailbox diagram,

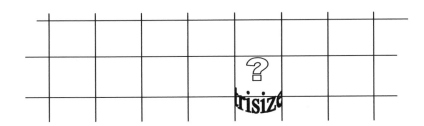

new mailbox for **triangle**

Now we need to change the **triangle** procedure so that we are using the variable **trisize** instead of the number one.

Can you guess how to do that? Let's try this:

```
to triangle :trisize
  ; draws a triangle
  repeat 3 [forward 50 * trisize right 120 wait 1]
end
```

In the command center, type **triangle 5**. You are calling the procedure and passing it a value (an argument). Did that work? Oops, it didn't!

We forgot! In the procedure, we need to tell the computer to get the *value stored* in **trisize!**

Use **:trisize** rather than just **trisize.**

```
to triangle :trisize
  ; draws a triangle
  repeat 3 [forward 50 * :trisize right 120 wait 1]
end
```

Now, in the same way, add a variable (you pick the name) to all the procedures except **Main.** First put the variable name, such as doorsize, in the procedure's first line preceded by a colon. Within all procedures, restate **forward** and **back** values as a number * 1, and then replace the 1 with **:doorsize** (or whatever). Don't use the same variable name in two different procedures. This could cause confusion for the computer. We want all our variables to be local—that is, we use the variable name only inside the procedure that creates it.

Test each procedure by typing the procedure name followed by a number into the Command Center.

square 2
climb.to.roof 2
triangle 2
door 2

See if the computer draws each one properly. Troubleshoot according to your error messages. Sometimes Logo doesn't like the quote marks you use. Make sure they are the double ones.

Now, let's pull it all together. Make your **Main** procedure into a list of procedures you are calling, with the input of 2 next to each, just like above.

Now, press the **Start** button. Does it draw a house that is twice as big? It should.

Can you change **Main** to draw a house that is half as big? Hint: use 0.5 for half; that means five-tenths, which is the same thing as one-half.

Show your teacher your half-sized house and your double-sized house!

Extra-credit exercise:

*Create a variable for **Main** that contains the value that will be used to re-size all the components. Hint: the first line of **Main** looks like this*: **to Main :housesize** . *To put a value into the variable, call **Main** directly from the Command Center, like this:* **Main 2** .

#11 Do the Logo Walk

Now, let's do some more animation. I would like to develop a procedure called **walk.**

From the file menu, open your project saved from an earlier lesson called **Square1**. Then from the file menu select "Save Project As" and save your project as **Walk.** Remember, this is the project where a horse was trotting in invisible squares. On the Procedures Page, your program should look like this:

```
====================
to Main
   cg
   cc
   pu
   talkto "t1
   setsh [horse1 horse2 horse3]
   repeat 20
      [square 30]
end

=====================

to square :length
   repeat 4
      [forward :length right 90 wait 1]
end

to Start
   Main
end
```

Our approach

We are going to experiment with making a procedure **walk.** We will start out with a general idea of what we want to do but we will build the procedure bit by bit as we see what works and what doesn't. And we will make mistakes along the way that we will learn from and use to make our procedure better.

After we do **walk,** I would like to do **jump**. Eventually, I would like to make a critter walk along and jump over things.

How do you walk?

In Main, edit the **setsh** line so that it looks like this:

> **setsh [dog1 dog2]**

Install the shapes **dog1** and **dog2** into your Shape Center. Make sure they are facing to the left. To change the way they face, double-click on the shape in the Shape Center, and then click on the flip icon [icon].

Let's actually sit down and think a bit before we start to write our **walk** procedure. I envision the turtle switching back and forth between two shapes as it moves along. This means that the procedure **forward** must be called more than once. We could call it twice, once for each shape, then repeat that sequence. We should include a **wait** command to slow down the action to where we can see it.

What about inputs to **walk**? What should we make as a variable? Well, how about making how far to go before changing shapes an input to the procedure?

Okay, enough thinking, let's code!

In the command center, type **cg** to clear the graphics, so we can start fresh. Then type in this procedure in your procedures page.

```
to walk :stepsize
  repeat 2
    [forward :stepsize
    wait 1]
end
```

and edit **Main** to look like this:

```
to Main
  cg
  cc
  pu
  talkto "t1
  setsh [dog1 dog2]
  repeat 200
    [walk 5]
end
```

In the **walk** procedure, you can see that we added an input to **forward**—the value in the variable **stepsize**. That value is passed from Main when the procedure **walk** is called, which now has an input. See how they are tied together?

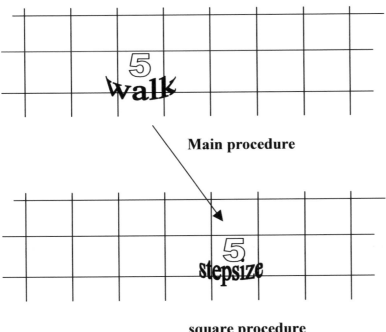

Main procedure

square procedure

Go to your Graphics Page and click on the Start button. How did it go?

My dog went backwards! Yours may be going up or down! We forgot to set the heading of the turtle/dog before we called **walk**. (Remember, the heading is the direction the turtle is facing.) My dog faces the opposite direction from my horse. We forgot one of our programming goals, which I repeat here:

It must work every time for every one. In other words it can't depend on the user doing things in the right order, or depend on the turtle facing the right direction or some other condition. It must account for and handle all those possibilities itself.

How can we do that? We'd like to point the turtle to the left, no matter what it was doing before that. So we need to set the heading, using **seth**, pronounced set-H for set heading. Let's try this: Add **seth −90**, or **seth 270** (same thing) to **Main.** (Do you wonder where these numbers come from? Take out a compass and look at the numbers around the rim. They add up to 360, the number of degrees in a circle. North is 0, so 270 is west. Or in our case, to the left.)

We are pointing the turtle's head to the left, no matter what it was doing before that.

```
to Main
   cg
   cc
   pu
   talkto "t1
   setsh [dog1 dog2]
   seth 270
   repeat 200
      [walk 5]
end
```

We want our **walk** to be able to work with any shapes in any direction. That is why we wouldn't add **seth 270** to the **walk** procedure itself. It also makes sense to put it before the **repeat**, because it would be inefficient to call it 200 times. I find the dog a little slow, so let's try increasing the step size to 10. Change **Main** and run your program again.

```
to Main
   cg
   cc
   pu
   talkto "t1
   setsh [dog1 dog2]
   seth 270
   repeat 200
      [walk 10]
end
```

There, I think that looks pretty good. Now let's do **jump.**

The jump procedure

Well, I guess the obvious variable in a **jump** procedure would be "How high?" or height. So let's get started:

```
to jump :height
   seth 0
   forward :height
   wait 1
   back :height
end
```

What do you think of this procedure? Do you think it will work? Let's add it to **Main** and give it a try. Here is the new **Main:**

```
to Main
  cg
  cc
  pu
  talkto "t1
  setsh [dog1 dog2]
  seth 270
  repeat 200
    [walk 10
    jump 10]
end
```

Give your program a try.

My dog just kept on going up!

Do you see why? In **jump**, we set the heading of the turtle to up (**seth 0**) but we never set it back again! In other words our **jump** procedure had the unpleasant side effect of changing the direction the turtle was headed. But how do we set it back to its original direction when it is finished jumping? Let's set the heading back to 270 (to the left) when it is finished jumping.

```
to jump :height
  seth 0
  forward :height
  wait 1
  back :height
  seth 270
end
```

Do you see how that works? Now try it.

I would like the dog to walk further before it jumps. How do we do that?

Let's try changing the size of the steps by changing **Main** as follows:

```
repeat 200
  [walk 100
  jump 10]
```

Well, the result is interesting, but the animation doesn't seem to work! What went wrong? Let's take another look at our **walk** procedure. Here it is again:

```
to walk :stepsize
  repeat 2
    [forward :stepsize
    wait 1]
end
```

What is happening is the dog is walking along, changing shapes once and then jumping. In order to get it to **walk** more than it jumped we made the stepsize larger (100). But this ruined the animation because I am not calling **forward** very often. What I really want is for the dog to walk along many steps while changing shapes, and then to jump. We need to revise our **walk** procedure so that we can control both the step size and the quantity of steps. Let's add another parameter (variable) to our **walk** procedure.

```
to walk :stepsize :qsteps
    repeat :qsteps
        [forward :stepsize
        wait 1]
end
```

Qsteps stands for quantity of steps. Now we can easily control the size of each step and the quantity of steps with each call to **walk**. Change **Main** to make use of this new power and try your program.

```
to Main
    cg
    cc
    pu
    talkto "t1
    setsh [dog1 dog2]
    seth 270
    repeat 200
        [walk 10 10
        jump 10]
end
```

There, that's pretty good! Change both inputs to **walk**. What happens? Change the input to **jump**. What happens?

The method we just used to develop these procedures should show you that finished projects don't start out as finished projects. You need to try things, adapt them to make them better and sometimes abandon them if you find a better way to accomplish a task.

When you see someone's finished project, don't forget that all projects start out the same way, a blank page. It just takes time and a large amount of perseverance to make them into masterpieces.

Save your work

Be sure to save your work as **Walk**.

We now have three movement procedures, but we are not really using the **square** procedure at this point. So let's delete it.

Here is the complete procedures page:

```
======================
to Main
  cg
  cc
  pu
  talkto "t1
  setsh [dog1 dog2]
  seth 270
  repeat 200
    [walk 10 10
    jump 10]
end
======================
to jump :height
  seth 0
  forward :height
  wait 1
  back :height
  seth 270
end

to Start
  Main
end

to walk :stepsize :qsteps
  repeat :qsteps
    [forward :stepsize
    wait 1]
end
```

Exercises

1. *Make a file called Buzz.*

2. *Use a bumblebee (bee1, bee2) or a hummingbird (bird1, bird2) as your character. Make the bee or bird fly across the screen and wobble downward and back up, and repeat the whole thing a number of times. Hint: the downwobble is an upside-down **jump**.*

3. *Be able to change the number of steps or wing movements between down-wobbles. Show a teacher the results of changing this.*

4. *For grins: replace the bee or bird with a snake (snake1, snake2).*

5. *Make the creature go forward, then wobble up and back, then go forward, then wobble down and back. Repeat the whole thing a number of times.*

6. *Extra credit: Make the creature fly like this repeatedly:*

Note: get out your compass and put the center of it at the spot where the turtle turns. Then you can read the number for the angle you need off the rim of the compass.

Save your work.

#12 A Jump Button

Eventually I want a **jump** routine that we can use to make a character appear to jump over obstacles. Right now we have the character jumping at regular intervals. For our next improvement, let's add a **jump** button so the character will jump when we click the button.

Load in your work

From the File menu, open your project named **Walk**. Then from the file menu select "Save Project As" and save your project as **Jump.**

In the Procedures Page, your program should look like this:

```
========================
to Main
   cg
   cc
   pu
   talkto "t1
   setsh [dog1 dog2]
   seth 270
   repeat 200
      [walk 10 10
      jump 10]
end

========================
to jump :height
   seth 0
   forward :height
   wait 1
   back :height
   seth 270
end

to Start
   Main
end

to walk :stepsize :qsteps
   repeat :qsteps
      [forward :stepsize
      wait 1]
end
```

Add a button

Our **jump** procedure seems to work very well when we call it from **Main**. Now I want the character to jump when I push a button! And only when I push a button!

First, ***let's add a button.*** In the icon bar, click on the finger pushing the button and then drag it to the page to make the button.

A dialog box pops up giving us the opportunity to type in the instruction that we want to run when the button is clicked. We could have different instructions and labels, but we won't do that. I want the label to be **jump**, so type **jump** in all the blanks that you have.

If you need to resize the button, drag an area on the Graphics Page that includes all of the button, then release the mouse button. The button should then have four handles (little boxes) on it which allow you to resize it. Put the mouse arrow on it, and push and hold the mouse button down while moving the handle to a different place. This changes the size of the picture. You can also delete the button when the handles are showing by pushing the **delete** button on the keyboard.

Drag the **jump** button down beside the **start** button. Try clicking on the **jump** button. What response do you get? The program tries to run our **jump** procedure directly, bypassing **Main**.

Hmm, we get an error message. Our **jump** procedure requires an input. But where do we put the input? I really don't want to have to go to the dialog box of the **jump** button to change the arguments for **jump** every time I want to try something different. Here's a solution—let's change the name of the **jump** procedure to something slightly different. Also, we want to change **Main** so that it no longer calls **jump**. Let's change the name of our **jump** procedure to **doJump** and remove the call to **jump** from **Main**. Make your procedures page look like this. I am italicizing lines that are changed:

```
========================

    to Main
      cg
      cc
      pu
      talkto "t1
      setsh [dog1 dog2]
      seth 270
      repeat 200
        [walk 10 10 ]
    ;get rid of the call to jump
      end

==========================


    to doJump :height  ; change the name from jump to doJump
      seth 0
      forward :height
      wait 1
      back :height
      seth 270
```

```
        end

        to Start
            Main
        end

        to walk :stepsize :qsteps
            repeat :qsteps
                [forward :stepsize
                wait 1]
        end
```

Try your program by clicking on the Start button. The dog walks (actually runs but we'll call it walks) across the screen. Click on the **jump** button. You get an "I don't know how to Jump" error message, because there is no longer a **jump** procedure. We renamed it to **doJump.**

Processes

There is one other thing to notice. Even though you get an error message, the little dog keeps on walking! We get the error message because when we click on the button, we call the procedure **jump** which does not exist any more. Doesn't that strike you as a bit strange that the dog keeps walking? We have an error, but the program keeps running! Let's try a little experiment. I'll call this one we just made Version 1 of the program.

Let's put the same error in **Main,** calling **jump,** and see what happens. Stop your dog and then edit **Main**, putting a call to **jump** back in, as follows:

```
        repeat 200
            [Walk 10 10
        Jump 30]
```

We will call that Version 2 of the program. Now, after the dog **walks** 10 steps, the program will call **jump**, which does not exist. On your Graphics Page, Click on **Start**. Sure enough, you get the error message but this time the dog stops.

What is going on here?

The explanation is that the Logo language has "processes." Each process is independent of another process. A process is almost like its own little program. When we click on a button we start a process. If we had more than one turtle moving along on the screen, each one would be running in its own process. In Version 1 of the program, clicking on the **Start** button started a process which had no errors and ran fine. Clicking on the **jump** button started another process which did have an error and would not run but did not affect the first process.

In Version 2, we put an error in the process that is started by the **Start** button and sure enough, the error stopped the process!

This was just to give you a brief idea about processes. Let's go back to Version 1. Take the call to **jump** out of **Main**.

Jump has a bug!

We need a new procedure **jump** which will be called when the button is clicked. Add this procedure to your Procedures Page:

```
to jump
   doJump 20
end
```

This gives us a way to pass a number to **doJump**. Now try your program. Well, it is fun. You can make the dog **walk** along and then, by clicking on **jump**, make him take a little jump and then carry on. This way we get to have the label we want on the button and we get to keep the program out where we can see it on the Procedures Page.

Did you notice something odd? Did you notice that the dog kept getting higher and higher after we click **jump**? It didn't seem to come all the way back down after a **jump**.

Well, folks, we have a bug in our program. Something is not right, and we need to debug our program. That is, we need to find what the error is. To debug a program, the first step is to find out exactly what is causing the problem.

Let's try to narrow it down. When the turtle just **walks**, it does not move higher.

Try stopping the **walk** (by clicking again on the Start button) and just clicking on the **jump** button. **Jump** seems to work just fine and **walk** seems to work just fine when they are run separately. But when both processes are running at the same time, we seem to have a bug in our program!

So, it only occurs when both processes are running at the same time. I would like to see the movement without the shape of the dog obscuring the turtle. In **Main,** put a semicolon in front of the **setsh** line, like this:

```
;   setsh [dog1 dog2]
```

The computer sees a line with a semicolon on it and considers it a comment, not part of the program. It is like all the words to the right of the semi-colon are invisible to Logo and just visible to humans. So we have just made this line invisible to Logo. (We "commented the line out." Programmers do it all the time.)

Let's turn the dog back into a turtle. Type a command in the Command Center: **setsh 0 <enter>.**

Now run the program. Seeing it this way, with the naked turtle, makes me a little suspicious of what is happening with **forward.** Sometimes the turtle points up, sometimes left.

Let's take a hard look at our two procedures and try to figure out what happens that is different, when both procedures are running at the same time.

You can see that both **walk** and **doJump** tell the turtle to move **forward. Forward** just means "go in the direction your head is pointing." So, if the **doJump** process is running, then the head is pointed up (**seth 0**). So during the time the **doJump** process is running, the **walk** process actually calls **forward** and increases the height of the jump! That is why the turtle edges a little higher each time, I THINK! We need to test this theory.

Looking at the code in **doJump,** we see that the turtle's head is pointing up right from the line **seth 0** until the line **seth 270** . If the turtle spent less time pointing up, would the amount the turtle kept climbing decrease? In other words, let's say the turtle spends time with its head pointing up, and the climbing problem decreases. Then that would confirm our suspicion that the problem is **walk** calling **forward,** while **doJump** has the turtle's head pointing up. It's like the turtle has two bosses who are issuing different orders, and the turtle tries to obey them both.

Let's also decrease the amount of time by getting rid of the **wait 1** line. "Comment out" that line too, as shown below.

```
to doJump height
    seth 0
    forward :height
;   wait 1
    back :height
    seth 270
end
```

Get the turtle walking and then click **jump** several times. On my system, that eliminates the "climbing up" problem! Unfortunately you can barely see the turtle **jump,** but we know that it is jumping.

Another way to test is to change **wait 1** to **wait 3** and see if it makes the problem worse. Try it.

Now we understand that the problem is that while the turtle is pointing up in **doJump, walk** makes it go higher. But how are we going to fix it?

Let's eliminate the use of **forward** in the procedure **doJump.** This might solve the problem. It would be nice if we could make the turtle jump without changing its heading at all. Then **walk** could make it go forward at the same time without any bad effect. As computer programmers, our next step is to check the Logo Vocabulary in the Help menu to see if there are any other built-in procedures that we could try.

Using ycor

Way down at the bottom of the Index are **xcor** and **ycor**. **Ycor** looks like a very likely candidate, so let's look it up.

Go to Help, then Vocabulary

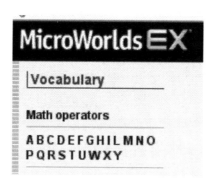

On the left side of the page, you see an alphabet to help us look up the word we are interested in. Choose y.

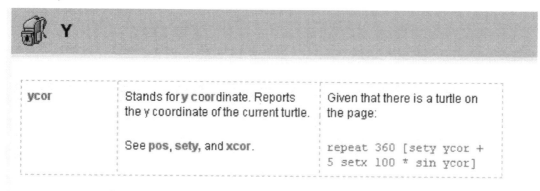

ycor	Stands for y coordinate. Reports the y coordinate of the current turtle.	Given that there is a turtle on the page:
	See **pos**, **sety**, and **xcor**.	`repeat 360 [sety ycor + 5 setx 100 * sin ycor]`

This tells us that there is a built-in procedure **ycor** that has as an output the y coordinate (height on the screen) of the turtle. There is another procedure **sety** which takes a number as an input and presumably sets the y coordinate.

How might this help us?

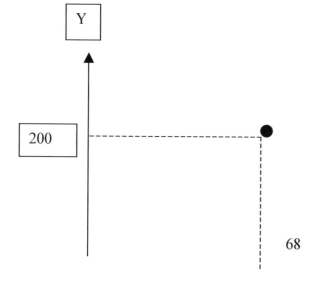

68

In this little picture, our dot has an address. Its "x coordinate" (sideways position on the screen) is 300. Its "y coordinate" (height on the screen) is 200. These numbers tell us just where we are on the screen, like a street address. It's just like Star Trek or Star Wars, reporting your position using coordinates!

Let's say x=300, y=200 is the address for our turtle. What if we move the turtle up on the screen a little way?

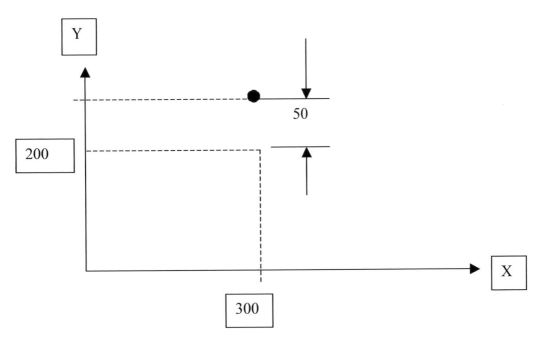

We moved the turtle upward by 50 units. So its y coordinate has changed from 200 to 250. Its x coordinate is still the same.

That is what we want to do! Tell the turtle to jump up by telling it to go from one position to the next. The second position has a y coordinate that is 50 steps higher.

But wait, how do we get the turtle to come back down to the same spot again?

We would know exactly where to tell it to go if we made a pigeonhole mailbox to save the first y coordinate and could pull that information out when we needed it. Let's:

- **make a variable and save the y coordinate of the first position**
- **move the turtle to a spot where we have added 50 to the y coordinate**
- **wait a little**
- **pull out the y coordinate of the first position**
- **and move the turtle back to that.**

Let's cast that into Logo. Can you do it on your own and then check your answer with mine? Turn the page when you are ready. But don't turn too soon! You will be cheating only yourself.

You're working, right?

Here's mine:

```
local "originalY
make "originalY ycor
sety sum ycor 50
wait 1
sety :originalY
```

We can now make a few more adjustments.

It is quite common to want to re-write a procedure on a trial basis, but you don't want to lose the old one, at least not yet. Here is what I do. I rename the existing procedure to, say, **doJumpOld** and write the new procedure as **doJump**. That way you do not have to search through your program to change all the calls to **doJump**. They stay as they are, only now they are calling your new version of **doJump**. Then, when we're sure we've made a good change, we can get rid of **doJumpOld.**

Here is my **doJumpold:**

```
to doJumpOld :height
  seth 0
  forward :height
; wait 1
  back :height
  seth 90
end
```

Make a new doJump on your procedures page, with the same first line as before. Add our code snippet from above, which allows us to:

- create a new pigeonhole (using **local**) and save the y coordinate (using **ycor**) of the first position
- move the turtle to a location where we have added the value stored in **height** to the y coordinate
- pull out the y coordinate of the first position from its pigeonhole
- and move the turtle back to that.

Again, write down what you think before you look at what I came up with on the next page!

```
to doJump :height
   local "originalY
   make "originalY ycor
   sety sum ycor :height
   wait 1
   sety :originalY
end
```

Does it work? How do you change the height of the jump? Remember, you do it by changing the number used when calling **doJump** from **Jump**.

I like it! I like our new version of **doJump,** and it has fixed the "climbing up" problem. Time to tidy up our program and save it. Here is my version**:**

======================
```
to Main
   cc cg pu
   talkto "t1
   setsh [dog1 dog2]
   seth 270
      repeat 200
        [Walk 10 10]
      end
```
=========================
```
to doJump :height
   local "originalY
   make "originalY ycor
   sety sum ycor :height
   wait 1
   sety :originalY
end

 to jump
   doJump 40
end

to Start
   Main
end

to walk :stepsize :qsteps
   repeat :qsteps
     [forward :stepsize
     wait 1]
   end
```

73

Exercises

1. Create a file called **hopyourname,** based on the work you did for this lesson. In it, add to your **jump** program a procedure called "**hop**" that:

    • Makes the dog hop sideways and back when you push a button called "**hop**." (This will be similar to **jump**.)

    • Does not use "**forward**."

    • Uses variables. Show your dog with two different sizes of hops.

2. Change your dog to a horse. Change the code so that the animal is facing right and walks forward when you push **start**.

3. Change the size of the animal's steps and the number of steps it takes when you push **start**.

4. Change the **walk** procedure so that it doesn't use **forward** either. Note that the animation won't be working, but the horse will move across the screen.

#13 Cool Animation

Load in your work

From the File menu, open your previous project named **jump,** the one with the running dog and the jump button. Then from the File menu select "Save Project As" and save your project as **jump2.**

In the Procedures Page, your program should look like this:

```
===========================
to Main
    cc cg pu
    talkto "t1
    setsh [dog1 dog2]
    seth 270
    repeat 200
        [Walk 10 10]
end
===========================
to doJump :height
    local "originalY
    make "originalY ycor
    sety sum ycor :height
    wait 1
    sety :originalY
end

to jump
    doJump 30
end

to Start
    Main
end

to walk :stepsize :qsteps
    repeat :qsteps
        [forward :stepsize
        wait 1]
end
```

Become a master of illusions

Programming sometimes involves creating an illusion. Often you will want to make a creature appear to walk or jump. Actually all you do is move the turtle, change the shape, move the turtle, change the shape. But to the user it creates the illusion that the creature is walking.

If you are using Windows, take a close look at your screen, especially the edges of the windows. It really looks 3-dimensional, doesn't it? It looks like the edge has some depth to it. But it is just an illusion. The screen is flat and two- dimensional. It is just the careful use of light and dark colors to create the illusion of shadowing that makes the screen look three-dimensional.

I want to make a program that makes it look like a creature is jumping over an obstacle. To do this we need to trigger the **doJump** procedure. I am going to program a color to call **doJump** and then plant that color in front of the obstacle. This will create the illusion that when the creature gets near the obstacle, it sees it and jumps over it!

Program a color

MicroWorlds has a really cool and useful feature that allows you to program colors. You can program a procedure to be called if a turtle touches that color, or a different procedure if the mouse clicks on that color. We will be using the turtle rule here.

Click on the paintbrush icon to see the **painting/clipart window.** Make sure the paintbrush icon at the top of the window is pushed.

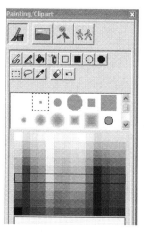

Right-click on a color in the spectrum, for example gray. A little button comes up that says "edit gray." Click on that button, and the color dialog box shown above appears.

You see that you can put an instruction inside this dialog box that the computer will run when a turtle touches the gray color. It goes next to the word "turtle" in the dialog box. Leave the line next to "mouse" empty.

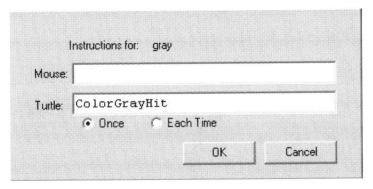

The color gray is an **object,** as is a turtle. An object has properties. In the real world, objects have properties. For example, if I jump on a trampoline, I bounce back. This is a property of a trampoline, not a sidewalk. In cyberworld, colors can have properties. If a turtle hits a color, it activates a procedure that you choose: bouncing back is certainly a possibility. We haven't written the procedure yet, but we will fill in the property in the dialog box anyway. In the white area next to Turtle: type **colorGrayHit** and click on OK. We will write this procedure in a second.

While you are in the Drawing Center and the gray color is selected, click on the spray can and spray a good solid gray splotch of color on the Graphics Page. Then go back to the Command Center. Make sure it is the same gray that you chose, no lighter or darker. Check the color numbers to make sure they are the same.

ColorGrayHit

Go to the Procedures page, and we will program the color gray. We want it to call **doJump**. Write the procedure **colorGrayHit** as follows:

> **to colorGrayHit**
> **doJump 50**
> **end**

Now go back to the Graphics Page and click on the **Start** button. Make sure your dog hits the gray splotch. Isn't that neat? My little dog jumps up and down a few times in the gray and then continues on its way. If yours isn't doing it, add more gray. You can do this by spraying more gray, or drawing a fat gray line, in the dog's path of course. If it isn't working, make sure you are spraying the **exact same color** as you programmed.

Jump a pond

Let's put a pond for the dog to jump over. You do this by hatching another turtle and placing him where you want the pond. If you have MicroWorlds EX, you will need to install the pond from the single-shape clipart window into the Shape Center now. In the illustration below, you see the pond at the bottom left of the image. Just drag it over onto an empty dot in the Shape Center.

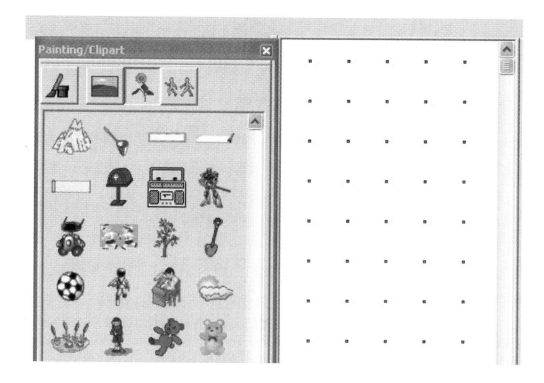

You can now go to your Shape Center, click on the pond, then move to the Graphics Page and click on the turtle. Here is the center of my screen now.

Try the program. For me, the results are pretty good, but we have two problems to fix. One is that it would be much better if the dog jumped forward, and with one jump cleared the pond. The other problem, which wouldn't be as noticeable if we fixed Problem 1, is that the dog disappears behind the pond. It would look better if the dog were in front of the pond. Let's fix the second problem first.

Who's on first?

In MicroWorlds, the most recently hatched turtle goes in front of any other turtles. Also the turtles are automatically named **t1**, **t2** and so on. In our case, this is not the order we want. The only way I know of changing this is to just accept it and change turtles. In other words, we will make our dog **t2** and our pond **t1**. To see what a particular turtle's name is, right-click on the turtle.

On the Graphics Page, drag the **t2**/pond out of the way and drag the **t1**/dog into the middle of the gray splotch. Then go to the Shape Center and be sure the pond is still selected. Click on the **t1**/dog. This should now make the first turtle, **t1**, look like the pond.

Our animation code will take care of making **t2** look like a dog, if we change the code. Go to the Procedures Page. We need to change our **talkto** line so that we are now talking to **t2**. Change **Main** as shown:

```
to Main
    cc
    talkto "t2
    setsh [dog1 dog2]
    seth 270
    repeat 200
        [Walk 10 10]
end
```

Give the program a try. There, that solves Problem 2. What do you think would be the way to solve Problem 1?

Go the distance

I think we need to either change our procedure **doJump** or to make a different procedure that both jumps up and forward. I like the first option of revising our existing procedure **doJump** and making it more flexible. We will try to make it so that it can be used both to jump up and down and to jump over something.

To jump over an object, the turtle needs to move up and also move forward a certain amount. We need a second input to **doJump** so we can control how far forward the turtle should move while it is jumping. Let's think like this:

> We will need two variables or mailboxes to store two values, height and a new one—how about distance?
>
> We'll set up a local variable, originalY, to hold the original y coordinate value.
>
> We'll put the original y coordinate in there.
>
> Now we'll set the y coordinate to a new number, the sum of the old one and the value in height. We'll wait a second.
>
> Now we need to move forward to clear the pond. How about going forward by the amount stored in the variable/mailbox distance? Then wait a sec.
>
> Then set the y coordinate back to the original value.

Can you set up some Logo code to match this line of reasoning? Try it. Then turn the page to look at mine, and see if yours is different.

Here is my **doJump**:

```
to doJump :height :distance
  local "originalY
  make "originalY ycor
  sety sum ycor :height
  wait 1
  forward :distance
  wait 1
  sety :originalY
end
```

We also need to change where we call **doJump**, to reflect two variables instead of one.

```
to colorGrayHit
  doJump 50 100
end
```

It works! Finally we have a great little procedure that can be used to make turtles jump over things.

You will notice that your **jump** button doesn't work right any more. To fix that, have it call **doJump** using two variables instead of one. How about this?

```
to jump
  doJump 30 30
end
```

Launching skaters

Before I end this lesson, let's have a little fun. Hatch another turtle and put it at the same distance up the screen as your gray splotch. This turtle is automatically named **"t3."** You can check this by right-clicking on it.

I would like to use the skater shapes-- **skater1, skater2 and skater3**--at the same time as the dog. If you have MicroWorlds EX, go ahead and install the skater shapes. How about if we modify the end of **Main** to add a section that says talk to **t3**, set shape to **skater1, skater2,** and **skater3,** and use the **walk** procedure to make it skate?

Program this on your own before turning the page. But don't spend too much time on it because there is a bit of information that we have not talked about yet.

(Which way did your skater go the first time you tried your solution?)

80

Here is my 'first try' which does not work right:

```
to Main
  cc
  talkto "t2
  setsh [dog1 dog2]
  seth 270
  repeat 200
    [walk 10 10]
  talkto "t3
  setsh [skater1 skater2 skater3]
  seth 90
  repeat 200
    [walk 10 10]
end
```

When you try this program, you will see that the dog continues to do its thing properly, but the skater never moves. Perhaps the dog is walking too many times. Change your **Main** as follows:

```
to Main
  cc
  talkto "t2
  setsh [dog1 dog2]
  seth 270
  repeat 5
    [walk 10 10]
  talkto "t3
  setsh [skater1 skater2 skater3]
  seth 90
  repeat 200
    [walk 10 10]
end
```

Try it and let it run for a few minutes. First the dog correctly does its thing and then the skater does her thing. If you follow the lines in Main, this makes sense. The repeat procedure causes the program to run the following list of instructions [Walk 10 10] over and over and then proceeds to the next line.

But what we really want is for a process to be launched making the dog walk and then for the program to continue to the next line and launch another process to make the skater walk, **at the same time**. This can be done using the built-in procedure **launch. Launch** has as an input a list of instructions to run as a separate process. Change your **Main** as follows:

```
============================
to Main
  cc
  talkto "t2
  setsh [dog1 dog2]
  seth 270
  launch [repeat 200 [walk 10 10] ]
  talkto "t3
  setsh [skater1 skater2 skater3]
  seth 90
  launch [repeat 200 [walk 10 10] ]
end
============================
```

There! Pretty cool, eh! Be sure to save your work. This program launches two processes that operate independently.

Exercise your skills

Learning how to program is a bit like learning how to ride a bike. Your teacher can tell you how to do it; others can show you how to do it; and you can read about it. But there is only one way to learn how and that is to do it. You have learned quite a few built-in procedures now and some programming techniques. Now you should consolidate your knowledge by actually putting these things to use.

1. *Save your file under **jump2**. Now save it again as **tornado**.*

2. *Modify the file so as to make the following things happen at the same time as the dog running and jumping and the skater skating:*

   - *Place another turtle, t4, in the shape of a castle in the lower right corner of the picture.*

   - *Yet another turtle, t5, takes the shapes of tornado1 and tornado2, and moves to the right toward the castle.*

   - *Spray-paint some turquoise blue (cyan) near the castle. When it strikes the blue, the tornado jumps over the castle.*

   - *When the tornado jumps, the castle turns into a cloud and then back into a castle.*

3. *In a new file, draw a maze with the drawing palette, using blue lines. Using the same idea as colorGrayHit, set up a turtle proceeding through your maze. Start it with a start button. You may want to use the procedure **random**, which delivers a random number. **Random 100**, for example, returns a number between 0 and 99.*

#14 Supercharge Your Browser

What is a plug-in?

If a company wants Web surfers to be able to see their program's files in the surfer's web browsers, then the company can write a plug-in to be added to the browser. The plug-in adds a further capability to the browser. Web browsers (Microsoft Internet Explorer and Firefox) have the built-in functionality to display different types of files such as html, jpg, gif and java applets. With plug-ins, you can extend the capabilities of your browser to view other file types.

The programmers for MicroWorlds have built a plug-in. If you download and install the plug-in (instructions to follow) then you can actually run a MicroWorlds project right in your browser, animation and everything! It is very cool.

Getting the plug-in

As soon as you say "download," a lot of people say to themselves, "Oh, that's too technical for me!" and leave. Did you realize that you successfully downloaded any text that you have read on the Internet? That's right, a page is "downloaded" from a Web server to your computer and, because it is an HTML file, your browser knows how to display it. Downloading just means moving from a Web server to your computer.

When you download an HTML file or a jpg or a gif, they are displayed in your browser. If you try to download an exe (executable) file, Internet Explorer and Firefox assume you want to save it to disk and will ask you where you want to save it.

I am going to walk you step by step through the process of getting and installing the plug-in on a PC. For a Mac, follow the directions on the plugin website.

First, go to www.microworlds.com. Select the icon at the lower left for downloading free MicroWorlds Web Player.

This leads you to a page where you choose which Web player to download. Do you have a PC or a Mac? Find the right download link and click on it. Save it to your computer. Install it.

After the plug-in is installed, you can re-start your browser.

Now Test It

You can find the project library at www.MicroWorlds.com. Play with these and guess how they work. Pick one to work on yourself.

Part 2: MicroWorlds Games

#15 Madlibs

We are going to work on a new project, a game called Madlibs. It will give us some more practice dealing with variables.

We are going to follow a defined set of steps in programming this. They are:

1. Decide on the goal.

2. "Sandbox" to acquire necessary knowledge.

3. Write pseudocode, which describes in English what we want to do.

4. Code.

5. Test.

6. Do it all again, that is, "enhance."

Probably you have played Madlibs before, not using a computer. First you write a story that has blanks in it. Then you interview someone, writing down a noun, the name of a vegetable, or whatever you need, using the person you are talking to as a random word generator. Then you put the words into your story. The result is pleasantly nonsensical, and you can both enjoy it.

To do the project, we need to follow our programming steps!

1. Decide on the goal

In this step you need to think about exactly what you want the procedure to accomplish. There are always a few little decisions to be made, and now is the time to make them.

We will capture words from the user, save them, and then plug them into a story that prints out on the Graphics Page. We will use our knowledge of variables. We want to create a variable that will capture a word typed in by the user. Then we will keep the words stored until time to use them. So we will need as many variables as there are blanks in the story. Here is our assignment:

*   Make a madlib using at least five variables.

*   Ask the user to give us words to put in the variables.

*   Print out a story using the five variables into a text box.

*   Make a procedure called **madlibs** that works with a **Main** and a **Start** procedure.

2. Sandbox to acquire necessary knowledge

This step is a *learning* step. Here you look at your goal and see if there are some aspects that you need to learn more about before you can write the code. If so, then you write some "sandbox" or "throw-away" code to teach yourself what you need to know.

We need to know how to accept words typed in by the user. Here is an example. Suppose we create and name a variable called **noun1**. Open a new file. On your Procedures Page, start a new procedure called **Madlibstest**. Then add a line to create a variable, **noun1**:

> **to madlibstest**
> **local "noun1**

Here's what we have created:

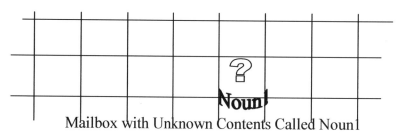

Mailbox with Unknown Contents Called Noun1

Now we type in this code:

> **question [What is your favorite animal?]**

This procedure, **question**, asks the user a question and gives space for an answer.

> **make "noun1 answer**

The procedure **answer** outputs whatever the user just typed. The procedure **make** gives the variable **noun1** the value of answer. Let's say the user typed "worm." At this point, the variable **noun1** would contain "worm."

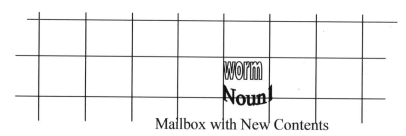

Mailbox with New Contents

Let's see what's going on. Your preliminary procedure looks like this:

```
to madlibstest
  local "noun1
  question [Please type in an animal name.]
  make "noun1 answer
  show :noun1 ;this means show what's in noun1
end
```

Go to the Command Center and type **madlibstest,** to run the procedure. Type in an animal name as requested. Does the computer show the animal name at the bottom of the screen? It is supposed to.

But let's make a text box and print our output in that. That way, we can use our game without using the Command Center. We would need that if we posted it on the Web. To make a text box, click the icon box with ABC or just A in it. Then click on the screen and size your text box to make it at least half the size of the screen. You can right click on the text box (then click on **edit** in MicroWorlds EX) and tell it to not to show the box name.

To print into the text box, we use the command **print**, instead of **show** to print into the Command Center.

Now we need to check for print in the Help vocabulary. Here's how.

In MicroWorlds 2.0, the **Help** button vocabulary index tells us about **print.**

For MicroWorlds EX, click on **Help**, and then on **Vocabulary**. A Web page pops up. In the upper right corner, you can choose Basic or Advanced. We will be needing Advanced, so choose that. Now choose the Vocabulary tab. Your Internet Explorer may block this page because it contains ActiveX programming, but it's local to your computer anyway, so click the popup blocker bar and allow the content. Now that you are on the Vocabulary tab, you can choose a topic from the left-hand menu to find the word you need, or you can click on the first letter in the alphabet that shows. We can click on P and locate **print**. Both MicroWorlds EX and 2.0 tell us something like this:

print word-or-list

Prints a word or list in the current text box. The text is followed by a carriage return and line feed sequence. See insert.

Example:

Given that there is a text box containing some text on the page:

print [The End]

The suggested format is **print word-or-list**. A *word* has a " mark right before it. A *list* is enclosed in [brackets]. So our input needs to have one or the other, " mark or brackets. Try these in the Command Center:

print "hello
print [hello]
print [[hello] [Mom]]

Can you get it to print "Hello out there!" ? Try it before you turn the page.

Our "Hello out there!" would look like this:

print [Hello out there!]

How do we get it to print out **what's in (:)** a variable? On the Procedures Page, let's try this:

to test
   local "noun1
   make "noun1 "me
   print [Hello :noun1]
end

Type **test** in the Command Center, and press **Enter.** Oops!! It printed "Hello :noun1" in the text box! That's not what we want! We want *what's in* **noun1!**

Let's look at a procedure called **sentence**. Here's what Help has to say about **sentence**:

sentence (se) word-or-list1 word-or-list2

(sentence word-or-list1 word-or-list2 word-or-list3...)

Reports a list which is made up of its inputs (words or lists). Sentence can take more than 2 inputs when sentence and the inputs are enclosed in parentheses. See list.

Examples:

show sentence "a "b

a b

show (sentence "hi "there [Bill])

hi there Bill

This is telling us to use this format:

print (sentence input1 input2 input3)

Notice the parentheses that include the word **sentence** and all the inputs. Each of these inputs needs to be one of these:

1. a word, with a **"** mark

2. a list, using [brackets]

3. "what's in" a variable, for example **:noun1**.

I want you to look at these commands, and guess which ones should work. Then test them in a test procedure. To make them work, first type this into the procedure:

   to test
   local [animal age] ;these are two variables
   make "animal "cow

88

```
    make "age 13
    ;put test sentence (shown below) here
end
```

To test each one, make sure you have a text box. Then type **test** in the Command Center to run the **test** procedure. You don't have to keep typing **test**; just put the cursor right after the word and press **Enter**. That will run it too. Here are your test sentences:

```
print (sentence "the :animal "ran)
print (sentence [The very large] :animal [ran through the woods])
print [Hello there] [How are you?]
print sentence [Hello there][How are you?}
print (sentence [Hello there] [How are you] [today?])
print (sentence [My age is ] :age [years.])
```

For grins, change the animal and the age in the variables and run them again. You could make a very large mouse run through the woods!

Now that we know more on this subject, let's get interactive and collect those variable contents from the user. In our **madlibstest** procedure on the Procedures Page, add these underlined lines:

```
To madlibstest
    local "noun1
    question [Please type in an animal name.]
    make "noun1 answer
    show :noun1
    print (sentence "hello "there :noun1)
    print (sentence [What are we talking about?] :noun1)
end
```

Now go to the Command Center and type **madlibstest**. Press **Enter.**

What do you get? Do some more experimenting.

We're well on our way to making a madlib!

Now, what if we want to create several variables at once? We'll need at least five variables. Let's guess that **local** might be able to help us. Look up **local** under the Help index. It says this:

local

local word-or-list

So we can use either a single word (with quote mark) or a list (with square brackets) as an input for local. For instance, we can say:

local "fred

to create one variable, or

local [fred sam bob]

to create several.

We need a list because we want to create five variables. Let's try this at the top of the **madlibstest** procedure:

local [noun1 noun2 noun3 noun4 adj1 adv1]

In fact, it is standard procedure in programming to create your variables at the top of the procedure, and then do the rest of the coding. So let's plan to do that.

We need one more procedure that allows us to talk to the user. Let's try **announce**. The Help menu tells us this:

> *announce*
>
> *announce word-or-list*
>
> *Displays the message in an alert box. Clicking OK closes the box. See* **question** *and* **answer**.

So the input for **announce** can be a list of words in brackets. Let's test this in the Command Center:

announce [Here is your madlib.]

Does it work? Let's add these ideas to our **madlibstest**. We can use these new tools: **question, print, sentence, local** using a list of variables, and **announce**.

```
To madlibstest
  local [noun1 noun2 verb3 adj4 noun5]
  question [Please type in an animal name.]
  make "noun1 answer
  announce [Here is your madlib.]
   print (sentence [One day the] :noun1 [took a walk in the rain.])
end
```

Planning

The next thing you need to do for our **madlibs** procedure is to write a simple story on a piece of paper or in a word processor. Underline five words that you will be erasing, but don't choose verbs (action words). Verbs are too hard to get right when asking input from the user. Separately, write down a question for each word. (Remember, the question needs to ask the user for a word of the same type, not exactly the same word, or the madlib won't end up being funny.) Keep the questions in order. Next to each question, write down a good variable name for that underlined word, for example, noun1, noun2, noun3, adj1, adv1, and so on.

3. Pseudocode

Pseudocode is just like program code except that it is written in English. It helps us make a quick and easy plan without worrying yet about getting details exactly right.

90

Go to the Procedures Page and type **to madlibs**, to begin your pseudocode. Put a semicolon at the beginning of the next line so we know it is pseudocode. First make pseudocode for creating and naming your variables. For example:

> **to madlibs**
> **;create and name variables noun1, noun2, noun3, noun4, adj1, adv1**

Your second line of pseudocode will ask the user a relevant question for the first missing word, such as "Please describe a feeling" or "Give me an adverb, such as slowly, quickly, heavily, etc." Write that pseudocode, with semicolon. For example:

> **;ask the user to type an animal name**

Your third line of pseudocode will take the word from the user and store it in the first variable. For example,

> **;store the animal name in a variable named noun1**

Do the same two things—ask the user for a word and store it-- for the next variable and the next until you have five variables. Write these lines of pseudocode.

Your next line of pseudocode will announce "Here is your madlib." Write this.

Finally we have the story-writing section. Write pseudocode lines for printing out your story into the text box, inserting the right variables in the right places. For example:

> **;print "There once was a noun1. One day the noun1 went to the park and saw a noun2."**

Now, show your teacher. Your teacher can compare it with the pseudocode in the answer key and give you pointers.

4. Code

Translate your pseudocode into code, that is, into Logo. In other words, after each line of pseudocode with a **;** in front of it, put a real line of code that says the same thing in Logo. Your code should be based on our latest version of **madlibstest**, earlier in this lesson. Look at **madlibstest** to figure out how to translate each line of pseudocode into code.

5. Test

Test your creation by typing **madlibs** in the Command Center. Then make a **Main** procedure that calls **madlibs** and a **Start** procedure that calls **Main**. Make a **Start** button. Does it work? Now you have a complete program. Check with the answers in the back of the book if you are having trouble.

Exercise

Make a second Madlib with a different story and different variables, totaling 7 variables instead of 5.

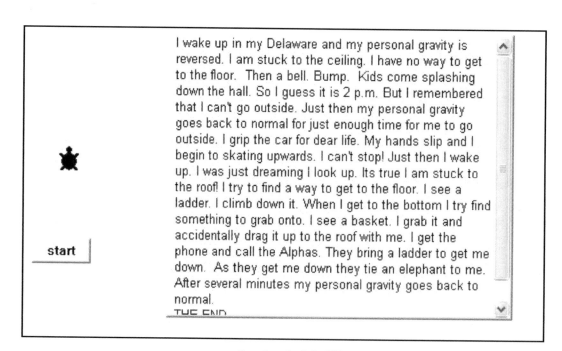

I wake up in my Delaware and my personal gravity is reversed. I am stuck to the ceiling. I have no way to get to the floor. Then a bell. Bump. Kids come splashing down the hall. So I guess it is 2 p.m. But I remembered that I can't go outside. Just then my personal gravity goes back to normal for just enough time for me to go outside. I grip the car for dear life. My hands slip and I begin to skating upwards. I can't stop! Just then I wake up. I was just dreaming I look up. Its true I am stuck to the roof! I try to find a way to get to the floor. I see a ladder. I climb down it. When I get to the bottom I try find something to grab onto. I see a basket. I grab it and accidentally drag it up to the roof with me. I get the phone and call the Alphas. They bring a ladder to get me down. As they get me down they tie an elephant to me. After several minutes my personal gravity goes back to normal.
THE END

Stephen's Madlib Results

#16 Madlibs II

Let's work on it some more!

Decide on the Goal

Now we want to add another procedure; we'll call it **intro**. It chats with the user a little and then asks whether the user wants to play madlibs. This way, we'll get some practice with the **if-then statement**, another element that is common to all computer languages.

Here's the pseudocode for it:

> **to intro**
> **;makes a dialogue box to ask "What's your name?"**
> **;says, "I like your name."**
> **;asks, "Would you like to play madlibs? Y or N"**
> **;if the user answers Y, then go to madlibs**
> **;otherwise, say "Bye!"**
> **end**

Sandbox to Acquire Necessary Knowledge

We need to learn about if-then statements. We want to do one thing if the user answers Y, and something else if the user answers anything else.

Let's consider this statement:

> **If it is raining, then you need to take your umbrella.**

The first part is a condition which we need to test. Is it true or not true? If it is true, then we take the action following, namely take the umbrella.

This is a type of statement that a computer can understand. We can write

> **if (it is raining) [take your umbrella]**

The (it is raining) condition has what is called a **Boolean** value: it is either true or false. (This is named after an English mathematician, George Boole.)

This type of situation where there are only two alternatives is very easily understood by a computer, which is really just a bunch of on-off switches (or T-F switches). So as the computer reads the condition, it will evaluate and assign a T or an F value to it. If the condition is true, it will execute the action. If it isn't true, it just goes on down to the next line.

Now, a computer inside a building might have some trouble figuring out whether it is raining. It would need to read sensors on the outside of the building. But there are many problems it can easily evaluate to T or F. For example, it can ask the user for a number, and it can test the number to see whether it is greater than 1.

Or it can ask the user for a letter, and test to see if the letter is a Y. In the case of our problem at hand here, we can type,

If (answer = "y)
　　[madlibs]

Pseudocode

I gave you some pseudocode already. Here it is again:

> **to intro**
> **; makes a dialogue box to ask "What's your name?"**
> **; says, "I like your name."**
> **; asks, "Would you like to play Madlibs? Y or N"**
> **; if the user answers Y, then go to Madlibs**
> **;say "Bye!"**
> **end**

Code

Let's make that into code.

Change **Main** so that it calls **intro** instead of **madlibs**. You're calling **madlibs** now from **intro**, not from **Main.**

Test

Now let's test it. First, let's put it into presentation mode. On the top of the Graphics Page screen is a series of menus, starting with **File** in the upper left. In MicroWorlds 2.0, select **Gadgets**, and under it, **Presentation Mode**. In MicroWorlds EX, look under the **View** menu and choose **Presentation Mode**. Your screen changes. (To get out of **Presentation Mode**, click on the black area around the screen.) Push the **Start** button and run through the madlib.

What happens if the computer asks if you want to play madlibs, and you type something besides Y? The computer goes on to the next line of code. Also, what happens after you go through your madlib and finish it? If you followed this pseudocode, you'll soon get the same thing both times: the computer tells you "Bye!"

But this isn't quite what I want. I want it to say "Bye!" only if the user types something besides Y and refuses to play. So the program needs more work.

Do it again

We need to sandbox some more. We want the computer to do one thing (play madlibs) if the answer is Y, and something else (say "Bye!") if the answer is other than Y. In most computer languages this is called an **If-then-else** statement. We would be writing something like this:

> **If (answer equals Y) go to madlibs**
> **else**

print "Bye!"

After the **else** is the secondary command, which is executed if the condition (answer equals Y) is false. **Else** is a shorthand way of saying "otherwise." This is the way it is in several other computer languages.

But in Logo, the if-then-else sequence is a bit nonstandard. Let's review: Logo has a procedure called **if** that has two inputs. One is the condition, evaluating to true or false. The other is the command to execute if the value is true.

if (condition) [command to execute if true]

If we look in the Help menu, we see that Logo also has a procedure called **ifelse** that has three inputs: the condition for evaluation to true or false, the command to execute if the value is true, and the command to execute if the value is false.

ifelse (condition) [command to execute if true] [command to execute if false]

Exercises

1. Use **ifelse** in your code and modify your game so that it follows this pseudocode:

;If (answer equals Y) go to madlibs, otherwise print "Bye!"

2. Invent a game called One Question (a very dumb version of Twenty Questions). Use these instructions below to write your pseudocode (lines of instruction in English that start with a semicolon, or ";"). You will need a **Start** button and a text box. You need procedures for **Start**, **Main**, **intro**, and **oneq**. **Start** calls **Main**. **Main** calls **intro**.

A procedure called **intro** asks the user's name and says it likes it. It asks if the user wants to play One Question. If the answer is Y, the computer calls for the procedure **oneq**. If it is not Y, it says "Bye!"

The procedure **oneq** has a local variable, **quiznumber**. The procedure puts the number 4 in that variable. Then the computer asks the user to guess a number between 0 and 10. The computer compares the stored number to the guess. If the answer is greater than what's in **quiznumber**, the computer announces "too big!" If the answer is smaller than what's in **quiznumber**, it announces "too small!" If the answer equals what's in **quiznumber**, it announces "You got it!" Then it prints a sentence reporting the number stored in **quiznumber**.

Construct your pseudocode from the instructions, putting semicolons before each line. Then after each pseudocode line, write a line of code in Logo without the semicolon. Test it and get it to work. Change the 4 stored in **quiznumber** to something else. Get a friend to play your game.

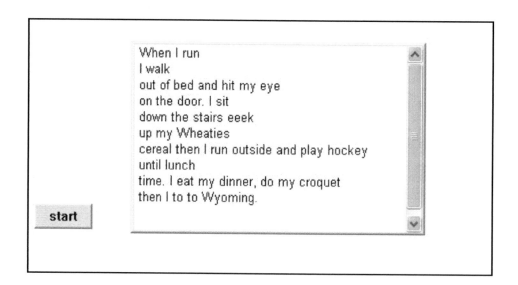

Lianna's Madlib

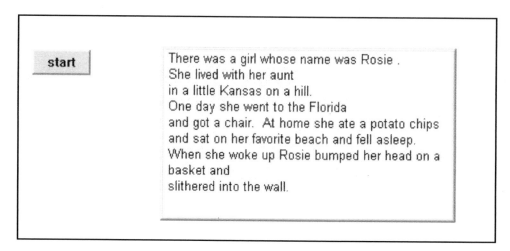

Elisa's Madlib

#17 Review of Animation Using Variables

Pull up your **Square** file, or type in the following:

```
======================
to Main


end
======================


to square
  repeat 4 [forward 50 right 90 wait 1]
end

to Start
  Main
end
```

Now it's time to add an action figure. I want you to add some lines to Main so it looks like this:

```
======================
to Main
  cc
  talkto "t1
  setsh [horse1 horse2 horse3]
  repeat 20 [square]
end
======================
```

If you have MicroWorlds EX, this won't work until you install the shapes **horse1, horse2,** and **horse3** into your Shapes Center, as shown on page viii of this book.

This is a simple animation. It uses **setsh** (for set shape) and a list of turtle shapes. Now, every time the computer calls **forward**, it goes back to the shape list and picks the next shape. We have chosen shapes that are similar, but the legs are in different positions. Our **square** procedure contains calls to **forward**, and **square** is repeated, so the computer keeps coming to **forward** commands inside **square** and changing the shape according to the list. The result looks like a horse running. The shapes can be shapes already given in MicroWorlds, or we can make them by clicking on a blank in the Shapes Center and using drawing tools.

Adding an Input to Our Procedure

It would be nice if we could decide how big a square our turtle should make. Then we would have a nice, general procedure that could be used anytime we want a square of any size. You won't believe how easy it is to make this improvement, now that we understand variables.

We want to turn our procedure **square,** which currently has no inputs and no outputs, into a procedure that receives one input. We do that simply by thinking of a good name for the storage spot for the input—how about length?—and putting it on the line that declares the procedure. We will use **what's in length,** written **:length.** Make the following change to **square:**

```
to square :length
  repeat 4 [forward 50 right 90 wait 1]
end
```

We just used a shortcut! Instead of using the instruction **local,** we put the new variable name in the first line of the procedure. This takes a spot in memory and names it **length** so we can store a value in it.

Again, using our mailbox diagram, we can see our variable.

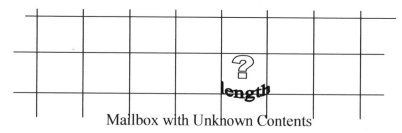

Mailbox with Unknown Contents

The neat thing is that we don't have to use **make** to put the value in. We pass the value to the **square** procedure when we call it. In other words, when we use the **square** procedure, we need to place an input next to it that will go into the mailbox. The code in **Main** needs to say, for example,

square 30

instead of just **square.**

When the computer gets to **square 30,** right at that point, a 30 goes into the mailbox named **length** and waits to be used by the procedure **square.**

So **square** now needs one input. Its jigsaw piece looks like this now:

Now we need to change **Main.** Instead of typing **square,** we will type **square 30.**

```
to Main
  cc
  talkto "t1
  setsh [horse1 horse2 horse3]
  repeat 20 [square 30]
end
```

Now you can try your program, and you will find that it works, but it really isn't any better than before. Our revised procedure **square** requires an input and gets an input, but it doesn't actually use it for anything!

Let's fix **square** so that it makes use of the variable **length**. We want the value stored in **length** to be used as the input to **forward**. Do you remember how? Take a minute to think about it.

Instead of saying **forward 50**, we'll say **forward what's in length**. Instead of "what's in," use a colon before the variable name. Change your **square** procedure as follows:

> **to square :length**
> **repeat 4**
>   **[forward :length right 90 wait 1]**
> **end**

Now, to find the input for **forward,** Logo must find the value stored in **length.** Where did that value come from? The value is stored there when Main calls the procedure **square** using a number.

Play with your new, more powerful **square** by changing this calling value, currently **30**. Officially this value is called an *argument*. (I don't know why. I'm not mad; are you mad?) Inside the procedure the variable is called a *parameter*.

You can also call **square** directly from the Command Center, for example by typing **square 200** and pressing **Enter.**

We have now finished a very good procedure that we can use any time we want. Here is my finished program, complete with lines setting off Main from the rest of the program, and procedures in alphabetical order:

> ==============
> **to Main**
> **cc**
> **talkto "t1**
> **setsh [horse1 horse2 horse3]**
> **repeat 20 [square 30]**
> **end**
> ==============
> **to square :length**
> **repeat 4**
>   **[forward :length right 90 wait 1]**
> **end**
>
> **to Start**
> **Main**
> **end**

Exercises

1. Test it! Put in different values for the line in **Main** that calls **square**. Use **square 40** and **square 60**.

2: Take the One Question guessing game you created in the previous lesson. Have the turtle do a little dance when someone wins.

Here's the pseudocode to add to your **oneq** procedure:

> **;if answer equals what's in quiznumber, do a jig**

You need to write a jig procedure. Use this pseudocode:

> **;announce that you got the right answer**
> **;talk to Turtle t1(talkto "t1)**
> **;put your pen down, pd (or pen up, pu)**
> **;repeat a number of times a list of commands that includes forward, right, etc.**

After each line of pseudocode, write a line of real code in Logo without the semicolon that does the same thing. Test your creation. If it doesn't work after you have worked on it for half an hour, look at the answers in the back of the book.

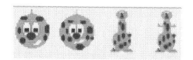

Stephen drew these shapes in the Shape Center for animations of characters from Veggie Tales.

#18 The Wandering Turtle

Programming Technique

Our next project is to build a procedure that makes the turtle wander around aimlessly.

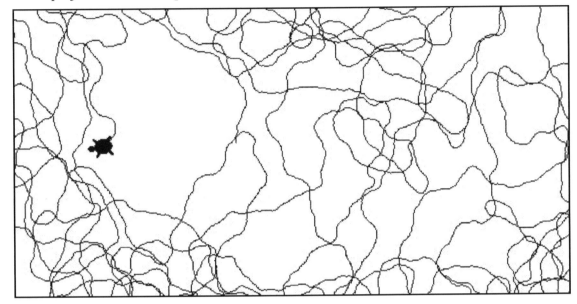

Decide on the Goal

We want our turtle to wander aimlessly. Let's have the procedure handle just one step in the turtle's aimless wander, and be called repeatedly. The procedure would slightly change the direction the turtle is going and then take one step in that direction. (Can you think of different plans for doing this?)

Sandbox to Acquire Necessary Knowledge

In our case, we want the turtle to change its direction some random amount. We will tell it to go right or left by this random amount. Random means "unpredictable." We need to learn more about this, so let's test some ideas, or sandbox.

In MicroWorlds, let's start a new project and add our usual **Start** button and code, like this:

```
===============================

to Main


end
===============================
to Start
  Main
end
```

Go to the Help screen and look up **random**. Remember how? In MicroWorlds 2.0, just click on H elp and Vocabulary. In EX, click on Help, then vocabulary, then on the Web page adjust the level from Basic to Advanced in the upper right, and choose the Vocabulary tab (allow the active content to get there if you need to). Now click on the letter R in the alphabet to the left.

Reports a random non-negative integer (including 0) less than **number**. The maximum number is 9999.

random number

Reports a random non-negative integer less than number.

Example:

show random 100

22

Random is a procedure that has one input, a number, and one output, also a number.

Random 100 generates a random number less than 100. Let's investigate. Write the following code on your Procedures Page:

```
===============================
to Main
  wander
end
===============================
to Start
  Main
end

to wander
  show random 100
end
```

Click on the **Start** button several times. We see random numbers, all less than 100, displayed in the Control Center.

In our **wander** procedure, we will want to change the direction of the turtle by a negative amount or a positive amount. **Random,** however, only outputs positive numbers. How can we make **random** give us numbers that are less than zero? Think about that one for a minute. Hint: we'll need to do some subtracting.

We need to do a little more sandboxing because we need some experience subtracting one number from another. A look in the MicroWorlds Help index turns up **difference. Difference** is a lot like **sum**. It requires two inputs and has one output. Its output is the result of subtracting the second input from the first input. Here is what the puzzle piece looks like.

Let's sandbox with **difference**. Change your code to the following:

> **to wander**
> **;show random 100**
>   **show difference 25 10**
> **end**

Notice that we put a ";" in front of the second line; this makes it a comment, not read by the computer. This is called "commenting out" some code. Try different numbers as inputs for **difference** until you are sure you understand **difference.**

Now, can you figure out how to make our procedure come up with random numbers, *half of which are less than zero?* (Hint: Use **difference** to subtract something from **random 100,** the random number less than 100.)

Don't turn the page until you think about it and try five solutions in the Command Center, using **show**. Here's how it will look, with the _ under the number you will supply:

show difference random 100 __

Here's a solution: **show difference random 100 50.** Fifty is half of 100.

We give **random** a number as input, 100. **Random** gives us an output number, say 76. We then subtract half the input number of 100 from the 76. Seventy-six minus 50 is 26, the number that will print out.

If the number **random** puts out is less than 50, for example 30, then the number that prints out is 30 minus 50 equals –20, a negative number. So about half the time, we should be getting a negative number.

Here's the code for this solution:

```
to wander
  show difference random 100 50
end
```

Do you have difficulty figuring out that line? When you "walk through" it, starting at the left, it is a bit easier. Just be sure to think of the outputs and inputs.

show - takes one input

difference - has one output; good, **show** needs that; takes two inputs

random - has one output; good, that is one of the two needed by **difference**; needs one input

100 - has one output; good, that is the one needed by **random,** so now **random** is happy

50 - has one output; good. That is the other of the two needed by **difference,** so now **difference** is happy and it makes **show** happy .

In other words, we are subtracting **50** from the output of **random 100**, and we are showing the result.

We'll be changing our turtle's heading. There are several ways to do this, but here's a simple one: how about a right turn? In the Help vocabulary, let's look at the procedure **right:**

right

right (rt) number

Turns the turtle to the right.

Example:

pd repeat 10 [fd 40 bk 20 rt 36]

If **right** has a positive input, the turtle turns to the right. If it has a negative input, the turtle turns to the left. So, half the time we will have a negative number, and so half the time the turtle will be turning left.

Write Pseudocode

Now that we have acquired some necessary knowledge, it is time to write this up as pseudocode. Here is what I want for the **wander** procedure:

```
to wander
  ;change the turtle's heading by a random amount
```

> **;move forward a certain amount twice (so the shape changes)**
> **end**

Pseudocode does not have to go into great detail, but it should be clear. In pseudocode, try not to use real names of procedures or numbers. Pseudocode also makes good comments to keep in your real code so you, or anyone else, can see at a glance what the procedure does. That's why I put a semicolon, ";", in front of it to show that it isn't real code. Typically, you would write the pseudocode sort of quick and rough as we just did and then revise it so it gets closer and closer to real code.

First, let's create and name a variable, **stepSize**, that will store the distance the turtle moves forward.

> **to wander :stepSize**

So when we call **wander** in **Main**, we use **wander 5** to give it an input number, 5, that is stored away. Then the computer sends the 5 to the variable **stepSize** in **wander**.

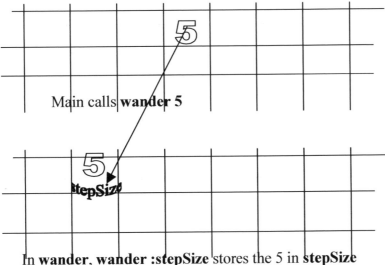

> **to wander :stepSize**
> **;change the turtle's heading by a random amount**
> **;move forward by stepSize, twice so the shape changes**
> **end**

There, that should be close enough that we can easily code it. Now let's move on to the fun part.

Code

Now, just do what our pseudocode tells us to do.

> **to wander :stepSize**
> **;change the turtle's heading by a random amount**
>
> _____
>
> **;move forward by stepSize, twice so the shape changes**
>
> _____
>
> **end**

We want to add lines to fill in the blank lines. (You don't need to type the blank lines in your Procedures Page.)

First, let's rewrite our pseudocode making it a little more specific. We are going to use a right turn.

to wander :stepSize
;turn right by a random amount which could be negative

_____

;move forward by stepSize, twice so the shape changes

_____

end

We'll add a line of code and underline it so we can see it.

to wander :stepSize
;turn right by a random amount which could be negative
<u>right random 100</u>
;move forward by stepSize, repeat twice

_____

end

This is a stab at the idea we were working on before. Now, let's try it. To test our procedure, type this line into the Command Center:

wander 5

Press **Enter.** What happens? Keep doing it. The turtle keeps turning—but always to the right! Hmm, what can we do about that? We forgot to subtract something from **random 100**, to make the result negative half the time. Do you remember what to subtract? Think about it before you turn the page.

106

You're working, right?

We will subtract 50 from **random 100**. Let's go over it again, in case we didn't digest it too well the first time. If **random 100** is 99, then 99 minus 50 is 49. If **random 100** is 49, then 49 minus 50 is −1. If **random 100** is 2, then 2 minus 50 is −48. So, about half the time we would get a negative number, and the turtle would be turning left instead of right. Remember?

Now, how do we encode that? We started with this:

We will have to use the procedure **difference**. What we want is the difference between random 100 and 50, or

> **difference random 100 50**

so our line of code turns into this:

> **right difference random 100 50**

Now, copy and paste this line from the Command Center to your Procedures Page, right after its pseudocode. I will underline it because it is new:

> **to wander :stepSize**
> **;turn right by a random amount which could be negative**
> <u>**right difference random 100 50**</u>
> **;move forward by stepSize, repeat twice**
>
> _____
>
> **end**

In the Command Center, type **wander 5** to test **wander**. Keep doing it. Does it turn right sometimes and left sometimes?

Now, let's finish it. Here's the next piece of pseudocode we are looking at translating:

> **;move forward by stepSize, twice**

Can you make a line of real code that does that? Use :stepSize for what's in stepSize. Don't look ahead while you think about it. It's exercise for your brain, stretching it like this. Again, test your line of code by typing wander 5 in the Command Center and seeing if the turtle does what you intended.

Test

Step 4 and 5, coding and testing, are usually all mixed together. You tend to code and test, fix and test several times in the development of a procedure. Now go to your program page and click on **Start.** We get an error message! Oops! We forgot to fix our call to **wander** from **Main**! Here is a revised **Main:**

```
================================

to Main
  repeat 60
    [wander 5]
end

================================
```

Now test it. Oops again! Our turtle is moving too fast! We forgot the **wait.** Also, let's put the pen down so we can see where the turtle has gone. We can also delete our pseudocode, now that we have it translated. Here is a revised **wander:**

```
to wander :stepSize
  pd
  right difference random 100 50
  repeat 2 [forward :stepSize wait 1]
end

to Start
  Main
end
```

Try it. Neat!

Exercises

1. In Main, adjust the **stepSize**. Test it.

2. Adjust the input to make smoother lines. How do you do that? How do you need to adjust the number subtracted from the random number? Test it.

3. Make the turtle's shape change as it wanders around. Hint: use **setsh** in **Main**. In MicroWorlds EX, remember to install some shapes to the Shape Center first.

#19 Enhanced Wandering Turtle

In the exercise for the last lesson, we adjusted the smoothness of the line the turtle is drawing. Do you remember how? We adjusted the input to random. Here's an idea: why don't we change the program so that the user can more easily make that change? Let's make the input to **random** into a variable. We can change its value by changing the number we pass to it from **Main**, just like we were doing by passing a value for **stepSize**.

Decide on the Goal—Again

Our goal before was "to <u>slightly</u> change the direction the turtle is going and then take a step in that direction." We will now enhance this goal.

New goal of **wander** : To change the direction the turtle is going, *based on a parameter to the procedure*. A parameter is a value passed to the variable. We already have one parameter, **stepSize**, passed from **Main**. We'll call our new one **dizziness**. Our call to **wander** used to be **wander 5**. Now it will be **wander 5 2,** for example. The first number goes into **stepSize** and the second number into **dizziness**.

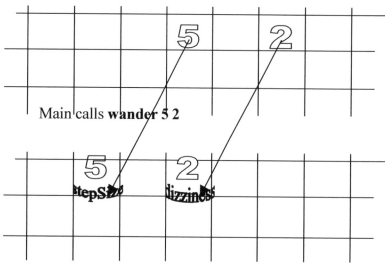

to wander :stepSize :dizziness stores the 5 in **stepSize,** and the 2 in **dizziness.**

This new variable will make **wander** more flexible. The turtle will be able to move along, more or less on track, and it will also be able to make more exaggerated turns, ending up going nowhere. All we have to do is change the input numbers for **random,** which changes the input number for the **right** turn.

Sandbox to Acquire Necessary Knowledge—Again

Here is our existing **wander**:

        to wander :stepSize
          pd
          right difference random 100 50
          repeat 2 [forward :stepSize wait 1]

110

end

The number that we are going to make into a parameter instead of a "hard-coded" number is the **100** which is an input to **random.** It is this number that determines how much the direction of the turtle is changed. However, the number **50** is tied to **100**. Remember, we had to subtract **50** from the result of **random 100** so that the turtle's heading could be changed by a positive or negative amount. How did we determine the number **50**? It was half of **100**, or half of the input to **random.** So we are going to need to divide our parameter in half.

We need to know how to divide one number by another number using Logo. A quick look in the Help vocabulary shows us that **divide** is not there, but looking further turns up **quotient,** as shown below. You remember from your math class that **quotient** is a fancy word for the answer to a division problem.

quotient

quotient number1 number2

Reports the result of dividing number1 by number2. See /.

Example:

show quotient xcor 10

We have used this same type of puzzle piece before with **sum** and **difference**. To sandbox we should type in a few lines directly into the Command Center to make sure we understand how it works. Try **show quotient 80 2.** That should do it for the sandbox.

Pseudocode—Again

In the pseudocode step, let's add **dizziness** as a variable in the top line of the procedure. Let's add this second line of pseudocode as a comment. I will underline the new stuff.

```
to wander :stepSize :dizziness
 pd
 ;turn right by a random amount up to dizziness
 right difference random 100 50
```

```
    repeat 2 [forward :stepSize wait 1]
end
```

Code—Again

Now we can write the code, then test it again.

Let's build it step by step. One way to do it involves creating another local variable (a variable used just in this procedure) to store the number that is half of what's in **dizziness**. Remember how to create and name a variable? We use **local**, like this:

local "halfDizziness

Then we need to put into that variable half of **what's in dizziness**, or **:dizziness**. How do we get half of **what's in dizziness**?

quotient :dizziness 2

That looks like this using puzzle pieces:

You see that **quotient** needs two inputs, one from **what's in dizziness**, and one is the number 2. It has one output, namely **what's in dizziness** divided by two.

Now, let's put that quotient into the variable **halfDizziness**, using **make**:

make "halfDizziness quotient :dizziness 2

Now, all we have to do is go back to our original code and substitute **what's in dizziness** and **what's in halfDizziness** for **100** and **50**. We had:

right difference random 100 50

Now we have:

right difference random :dizziness :halfDizziness

So our code looks like this now. I am underlining the changes.

to wander :stepSize :dizziness
  pd
  <u>**local "halfDizziness**</u>

```
;turn right by a random amount up to dizziness
make "halfDizziness quotient :dizziness 2
right difference random :dizziness :halfDizziness
repeat 2 [forward :stepSize wait 1]
end
```

Test

Now you can play with, I mean test your procedure. Here is my complete program:

```
============================
to Main
  cc
  repeat 60 [wander 5 10]
end
============================

to Start
  Main
end

to wander :stepSize :dizziness
  pd
  local "halfDizziness
  ;turn right by a random amount up to dizziness
  make "halfDizziness quotient :dizziness 2
  right difference random :dizziness :halfDizziness
  repeat 2 [forward :stepSize wait 1]
end
```

Exercises

*In the line in **Main** that calls **wander**, try these values for **wander**'s arguments: 5 & 10, 5 & 30, 5 & 300. What is happening to the turtle's dizziness, or change of heading?*

*Now, in the line in **Main** that calls **wander**, try these values for **wander**'s arguments: 5 & 10, 10 & 10, 50 & 10, 100 & 10. What is happening to the turtle's step size?*

What do you need to do to make the turtle buzz crazily, moving fast and turning widely? Say it and do it.

*Can you find any values for **dizziness** that cause an error? If you do, what do you think we should do about it?*

*Figure out a way to re-code so that we aren't using the local variable, **halfDizziness**, but get the job done anyway.*

#20 Maze I

Decide on the Goal

Now we want to make an interactive game where a turtle, **t1**, is wandering through a maze, moving in the direction the user indicates. The user will use the arrow keys. When the user presses an arrow key, the turtle will move in that direction a few steps. To get the turtle to go a long way, the user will need to press the button a lot of times.

Open a new file. Using the drawing center, we will draw some maze lines. In the next lesson, we will add capability. When the turtle bumps into a maze line, the user loses and has to start over. The user wants to get the turtle through the maze to a destination. How about a second turtle dressed up as a castle (or a hut)? Eventually we will add roving spiders that want to "get" our turtle, and teleporter booths that send the turtle to some other spot in the maze.

Nicole's Maze

Draw up a Plan

This time, we are going to add a step: draw up a plan. We'll make a flow chart. A flow chart is a visual plan of what we are going to do. You read it from top to bottom; the program flows from one box to the next down the chart, with diamonds indicating decision points. Here is a start for our flow chart for the beginning part of the maze:

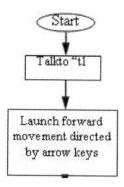

Sandbox for Necessary Knowledge

We want to move and turn the turtle by pushing the arrow keys. We'll need a lot of new information to figure out how to do this. First, how will we collect information from the keyboard?

Readchar is a built-in procedure that "reads" the input from the keyboard. Let's check to see if it works. In the Command Center, type

> **show readchar**

and hit the **Enter** key. Now move your mouse arrow up to the graphics window and click there. Hit a letter key. Does the letter appear in the Command Center? It should. Put your cursor at the end of the **show readchar** line and press **Enter** again, to do it again. Now press one of the arrow keys. Oops! In the Command Center, we don't see an arrow; we get some symbol like &! This will vary depending on whether you are using a Mac or a PC. What's going on here?

Readchar is reading the character, but it is storing its information as a number! Then it is pulling the number out and using a code to figure out what it is, and it's getting mixed up about the arrow keys!

When you play at writing spy codes, you assign a number to each letter of the alphabet. It turns out there is a code like that built into computers. It's the ASCII code, which stands for the **A**merican **S**tandard **C**ode for **I**nformation **I**nterchange, a code that assigns a number to each character. The problem is, it isn't an entirely standard code. The Mac and PC people use different code numbers for certain keys like arrow keys.

Logo has a built-in procedure called **ascii**. This procedure takes keyboard input from **readchar** and reports an ASCII code number for it.

Let's test this **ascii** procedure. In the Command Center, type

> **show ascii "L**

We're asking the computer to type the ASCII code for upper-case L in the Command Center. We get this response: **76**. This is the ASCII code for upper-case L.

Now, can you tell me the ASCII code for T? for the number 8? The letter H? h?

What we are most interested in is the codes for the arrow keys. But we can't type arrows into the Command Center. Can you figure out a way to get the computer to **show** the ASCII code in the Command Center for an arrow key? Hint: use **ascii** and **readchar**. Think about it and turn the page.

116

You're working, right?

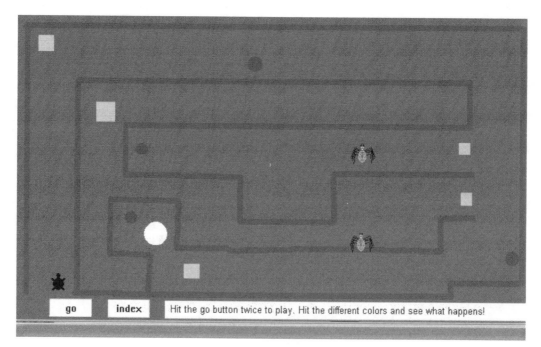

Hannah's Maze

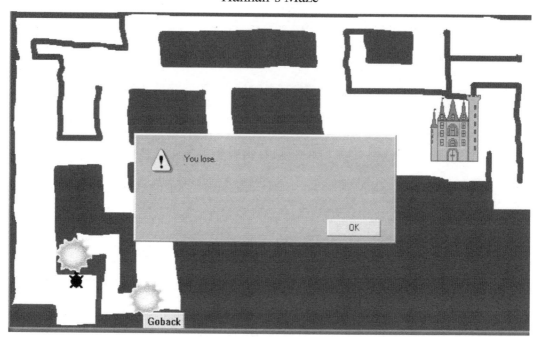

Robert's Maze

118

What we need is to use the procedure **ascii** to look at input from the keyboard delivered by **readchar.**

Let's try this:

show ascii readchar

Then press **Enter**, move the cursor to the graphics window and click, and push any key. What number do you get? Do it again and press an arrow key. What number do you get?

We are interested in a very limited set of ASCII numbers: those that represent the arrows on our keyboard. Those numbers are different for Macintosh and PC. So we will set up a code system that works on either a Mac or PC keyboard. What it boils down to is this: 28 and 37 can be left, 29 and 39 can be right, 30 and 38 can be up, and 31 and 40 can be down.

Directing the Turtle's Head

First we will write a procedure to direct the turtle which way to point its head. We'll call the procedure **direct.**

In **Main**, **readchar** will pick up the keyboard input. Then **Main** will pass the keyboard information to **direct**. How will it do that? Do you remember how to pass information around in a program?

A variable will do the job nicely—a little pigeonhole to hold the information. **Main** will put the **readchar** information in the variable, and **direct** will pull it out, evaluate it, and use it. Let's call the variable **key.**

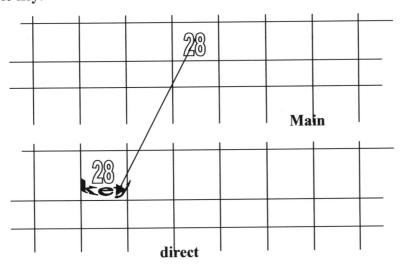

Main uses **readchar** to read "28" as the code for the key pressed. Then **Main** calls **direct** and sends it the value, storing it in the variable **key.**

Now our flow chart looks like this:

119

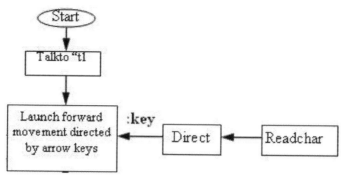

We will name the variable in the first line of the procedure **direct**, like this:

> **to direct :key**

When we call **direct** in **Main**, we would normally pass a number to it, like this:

> **to Main**
>
> **...**
>
> **direct 30**
>
> **...**
>
> **end**

But this time, we'll use **readchar** instead of the number 30. That way, whatever the keyboard input is will go into the variable, like this:

> **to Main**
>
> **...**
>
> **direct readchar**
>
> **...**
>
> **end**

In **Main**, we will read the keyboard input using **readchar** and then pass it to the procedure **direct**, storing it in the variable **key**. In **direct** we will evaluate it using **ascii** to see what the code number is. Then we will turn the turtle's head that way.

Here is our pseudocode for **direct**:

> **;If the code number is for the up arrow, set the turtle's heading to up (0).**
>
> **;If the code number is for the down arrow, set the turtle's heading to down (180).**
>
> **;If the code number is for the right arrow, set the turtle's heading to right (90).**
>
> **;If the code number is for the left arrow, set the turtle's heading to left (-90).**

It looks like we need four if-then statements, one for each arrow. But we actually need eight, because for each arrow key there are two possible code numbers (one for Mac, one for PC). Here is our finished code:

> **to direct :key**
>
> **if (ascii :key) = 28 [seth 270 fd 1]**
>
> **if (ascii :key) = 29 [seth 90 fd 1]**

120

```
    if (ascii :key) = 30 [seth 0 fd 1]
    if (ascii :key) = 31 [seth 180 fd 1]
    if (ascii :key) = 37 [seth 270 fd 1]
    if (ascii :key) = 39 [seth 90 fd 1]
     if (ascii :key) = 38 [seth 0 fd 1]
    if (ascii :key) = 40 [seth 180 fd 1]
    if (:key = "s) [stopall] ;this means stop the program
end
```

Copy this procedure into your Procedures Page; it will be your starter. You'll also need to create:

- a **go** button in the graphics window

- on the Procedures Page a **go** procedure that calls **Main**

- a **Main** procedure. We will talk about that next.

Pseudocode

We will work in this way: we will create pseudocode that solves our problem. Then we will translate lines of pseudocode into Logo, then test. We will build the program by doing this over and over, adding in features as we go.

Here's some pseudocode to start with:

```
to Main
  ;talk to turtle 1
  ; launch a process that repeats many times a call to go forward a little bit
  ;use readchar to collect info from the keyboard, and also
  ;call direct, passing to it the information collected by readchar
end
```

First, we'll work on the first line of pseudocode. We'll need more information on **launch**. Do you remember the **launch** procedure from *Book 1?*

The Help vocabulary tells us this about **launch:**

launch word-or-list-to-run

*Runs the input as an independent parallel process. If the process is launched from the Command Center, the cursor reappears immediately. Use cancel, the Cancel menu item, the Stop All menu item, or Ctrl+Break to stop the process. See also **forever**.*

Example:

launch [glide 1000 1]

Type the next instructions while the turtle is gliding.

rt 90

lt 90

Look at the very top of the entry: *launch word-or-list-to-run*. What this means is that we need to use a word or a list as input for **launch**. (Remember, a **word** starts with a ", and a **list** is enclosed in [brackets like these]. **Launch** starts a process that we need to stop separately. I **find** it works best to **launch** something also using the **repeat** command, along with **forward.**

Now, we need a line of code that does all of these things:

> **;launches a process that repeats many times a call to go forward a little bit**
> **;uses readchar to collect info from the keyboard**
> **;calls direct, passing to it the information collected by readchar.**

Can you think of one? Work on it before you turn the page.

Crystal's Maze. The bee tries to get to the moon!

You're working, right?

Here is mine:

launch [repeat 2000 [forward 3 direct readchar]]

Do you see how it works? Let's look at it from right to left. **Readchar** is taking one character of input from the keyboard. **Direct** is the procedure we made which needs one input (the keyboard character) and uses it to set the turtle's heading. Now, we have a little list of commands: go forward 3, and then change the turtle's heading using **direct** and the keyboard input. We will repeat this little set of commands 2,000 times, and we'll launch the whole process. This means that it will operate independently of other processes we might also launch.

Here's our next version of **Main**. I have underlined the new code.

> **to Main**
> **;talk to turtle 1**
> **;launch a process that repeats many times a call to go forward a little bit**
> **;use readchar to collect info from the keyboard**
> **;call direct, passing to it the information collected by readchar.**
> <u>**launch [repeat 2000 [forward 3 direct readchar]]**</u>
> **end**

Now, add a line of code to match the pseudocode for talking to turtle 1. Add the code for **to direct**, given earlier.

Now we have a program. Does it work?

Let's draw a maze to go with it. On your graphics page, Page1, make a **go** button (using the icon that looks like a finger pushing a button). Using the drawing center under the paintbrush icon, draw some thick red lines or curves for your maze. <u>Make sure you are using thick red lines with color 15, to match the code I will give you.</u> Pause the mouse over the color in the Drawing Center to be sure. You can make the maze more difficult by placing the lines close together. Go to Presentation Mode under the View menu in MicroWorlds EX, and in MicroWorlds 2.0 under the Gadgets menu. (To leave presentation mode, click or double-click on the black border.) Press the go button, and then start pushing the arrow keys to advance the turtle. Does it work? Work on yours before you look at mine on the next page. Be sure you use Presentation Mode for these mazes; otherwise they may not work properly. If your pen is still down, use the Command Center to tell the turtle pen up, or **pu.**

```
===============
to Main
 ;talk to turtle 1
 talkto "t1
  pu
 ;launch a process that repeats many times a call to go forward a little bit
 ;use readchar to collect info from the keyboard
 ;call direct, passing to it the information collected by readchar.
 launch [repeat 2000 [forward 3 direct readchar ] ]
end
===============
to direct :key
 if (ascii :key) = 28 [seth 270 fd 1]
 if (ascii :key) = 29 [seth 90 fd 1]
 if (ascii :key) = 30 [seth 0 fd 1]
 if (ascii :key) = 31 [seth 180 fd 1]
 if (ascii :key) = 37 [seth 270 fd 1]
 if (ascii :key) = 39 [seth 90 fd 1]
 if (ascii :key) = 38 [seth 0 fd 1]
 if (ascii :key) = 40 [seth 180 fd 1]
 if (:key = "s) [stopall]
end

to go
 Main
end
```

We have a maze starter now, but we have more to learn for this project.

125

#21 Maze II: Win or Lose?

Our starter maze does part of the assignment: it moves the turtle through some lines we have drawn, based on input to the keyboard's arrow keys. Now we want to do this part of the assignment: when the turtle bumps into a maze line, the user loses and has to start over.

Draw up a Plan

In our flow chart, we will need a diamond-shaped decision box as the next item down from the launch step. The decision box means the computer will decide whether a condition is true. If it is true, it goes down to the next steps (telling the user "you lose" and resetting the game). If it is false, it repeats the previous step. Like this:

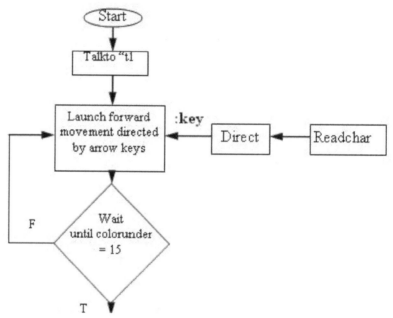

The condition will be this: did t1 run into a maze wall? Or more specifically, is its "colorunder" 15 for red?

First, More Sandboxing!

We need to learn more about some Logo procedures.

Colorunder is a procedure which has as output the number of the color the turtle is running into. So if the turtle runs into a **red** maze wall, the code can be detecting that by checking to see if **colorunder = 15.**

If **colorunder = 15** is true, we want to go on to the next step: announcing, "You lose."

Since we have launched a continuing process, though, we won't use

> **if (colorunder=15)**

That would only check once.

We have to use another procedure, **waituntil.**

126

The Help vocabulary tells us this about **waituntil:**

waituntil true-or-false-list-to-run

Tells MicroWorlds to wait until true-or-false-list-to-run is true before running another instruction. The input must be an instruction list that reports either true or false when it is run.

The input for **waituntil** is a list, so it is in brackets. The input must be something that evaluates to true or false. All this means that our code needs to:

> **;launch a process that keeps going**
> **;waituntil [something is true]**
> **;announce "You lose!"**

First, let's eliminate our previous pseudocode. It seems to be getting in the way. Now we have:

> **to Main**
> **talkto "t1**
> **launch [repeat 2000 [forward 3 direct readchar]]**
> **end**

Now, let's add some new pseudocode. We already have a line of code that launches the process. So now we need to put in the pseudocode for two more lines.

> **to Main**
> **talkto "t1**
> **launch [repeat 2000 [forward 3 direct readchar]]**
> **;wait until the color under the turtle is color 15**
> **;announce "You lose!"**
> **end**

You need to translate the new lines into real code and put them under the pseudocode lines. Use **colorunder, waituntil,** and **announce.** Put yours together before you turn the page.

Your new code should look like this:

waituntil [colorunder = 15]
announce [You lose!]

More Pseudocode

Now we need more pseudocode, inserted after the **waituntil** line. We want to return the turtle to its starting point with head up.

Write in the pseudocode for this, and then turn the page to check it against mine.

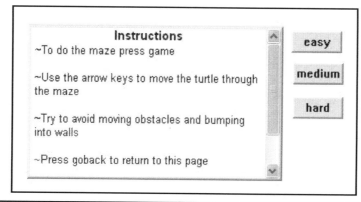

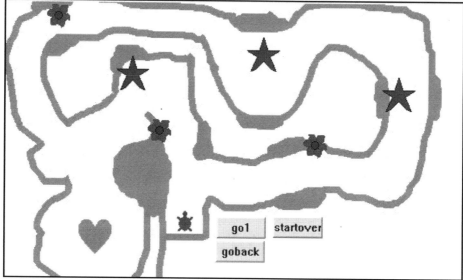

Elisa's Maze. Turtle tries to get to the heart of things.

You're working, right?

to Main
talkto "t1
launch [repeat 2000 [forward 3 direct readchar]]
waituntil [colorunder = 15]
announce [You lose!]
;reset the game: move the turtle to a position above your go box and
;set the turtle's heading to 0
end

Our Plan

The plan now looks like this:

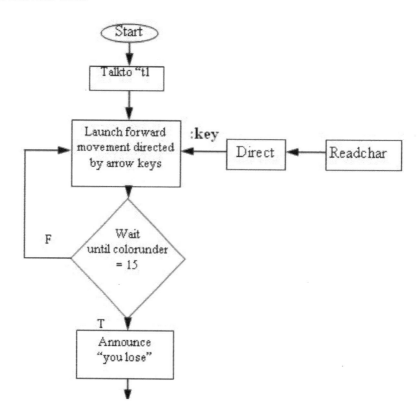

Some More Sandboxing

We need to make a **reset** procedure that returns **t1** to a place above your **go** button and sets its heading to zero. Should it include "You lose"? I think not. That way we can use the **reset** procedure both when we lose and when we win.

Here is your pseudocode:

> **to reset**
>   ;return t1 to a place above your "go" button
>   ;set its heading to zero
> **end**

We need to know a few more Logo procedures. How will we move the turtle to a position above the **go** button? **Setpos** will set the turtle's position. Look it up in the Help vocabulary to see how to use it. If you forgot how, go to page 22 of this book. You need to know the coordinates of the position you want (numbers representing distance to the right and distance up from the center of the screen). But what are the coordinates of the spot above your **go** button? That will be different for each maze.

To find the coordinates of the position you want, move the turtle there using your mouse—pushing and holding down the mouse button to move the turtle around. Then go to the Command Center and type **show pos**. Note that in this case there is a space in the middle: **show** is the procedure, **pos** is the input. This will tell you the coordinates of that spot. Put those coordinates into your line using **setpos** (no space). Use the format on **setpos** from the Help vocabulary.

Now, translate that to Logo, and call **reset** from **Main**. You have a basic maze! Test your creation and tinker with it until it works. Remember to use Presentation Mode.

Exercises

Add these enhancements. First, add pseudocode to your code. Then translate it to Logo.

1. Make a second turtle as the destination in the maze. Use the turtle-hatching icon. This will be t2. Put a castle shape on t2. This is easy in MicroWorlds 2.0. Just click on the shape in the Shape Center, and then on the turtle. To do this in MicroWorlds EX, install a castle shape from the single-shape collection under the flower icon in the painting/clipart window. Click on the castle shape and then on t2. Now shrink t2 down, using the magnifying glass with the minus sign. That way we can see the t1 animation.

2. Look up **when** and **touching?** in the Help vocabulary.

   Create a line in **Main** that changes the shape of **t1** when it touches **t2**. We want this to happen *before* the ending sequence—where the computer is waiting for the turtle to run into a red line to reset the game. Where should the new line of code go? Sketch the flow chart we have so far and add this diamond-shaped decision box to it in the right place.

3. Make a procedure called **win** that provides a reward for the winner—the one who reaches the maze destination. First it will announce "You win!" Next, how about an animation for the winner? Make this procedure change the shape of **t1** into a cloud, wait a little, and then change **t1** into another shape. If you have MicroWorlds EX, install the cloud shape from the single-animations collection (under the flower icon in the painting/clipart window). Also install some other shapes. To find the name of a shape, pause the mouse over a shape to see its name and number. You can use either the name (for example, **bee1**) or the number (**11**) to call it.

   In the **win** procedure, remember to talk to **t1**, then use **setsh**, wait a bit, and use **setsh** again.

   Test it by typing **win** in the Command Center, and pressing **Enter**. Once you get that working, call it from **Main**. You will need to change the line in **Main** that uses **when** and **touching?**

4. Now, make some adjustments to **win**. Change it so that you choose a shape *randomly* the second time you call **setsh**. Use **random** as input. Look up **random** before you use it to call shapes randomly. You take advantage of the fact that the shapes all have numbers.

   In MicroWorlds EX, these numbers come from the slot in the Shape Center where you installed the shape. So fill up the first 9 slots in your Shape Center with your favorite shapes. Then you will use 10 as your input for **random**.

   In MicroWorlds 2.0, you don't have to install any shapes – they are already installed. You just have to choose a number as input for **random** that makes sense based on what the shape numbers are; an input of 50,000 won't get you anywhere!

   Enhance **win** and **reset** so that after the turtle changes shapes upon winning, the turtle is returned to its turtle shape and goes back to its starting place. Now, play with your game! Save it as Mymaze. We will pick up here with the next lesson.

5. Draw additions to our flow chart to describe what we have made so far. You will want to make two pathways coming down from the one box that says "launch forward movement directed by arrow keys," to show that two things are happening at the same time: the **waituntil** and the **when**, and both can lead to the end of the game. Once you try a sketch, take a look at mine in the answer key.

Prince/Princess Project:

Save a separate version of the maze we have been working on, to make changes just for this project. Let's imagine our turtle is a prince or princess changed into a turtle by a witch. The turtle really wants to get to the castle at the center of the maze in order to be changed back into a prince or princess. Ask the user whether the user would prefer a prince or princess. Store this information in a variable and then use it to change the turtle into a boy or a girl, as appropriate to the choice, when the turtle reaches the castle.

Hints for **Main**: First, create a variable called **preference** to use within **Main**, using **local**. If you can't remember how to use **local**, look it up in the Help vocabulary (see page 15). You will also need to use **announce**, **question**, and **ifelse**. Look those up too, to jog your memory. If the user answers B for boy, you will need to make the value in the variable preference match the shape number for boy. Otherwise, you need to make the value match the shape number for girl. If you have MicroWorlds EX, be sure to download shapes to your shape center to use for a boy and a girl for your winning turtle to be. Remember what the shape numbers are and use them in your code.

Hints for **win**: Change **win** so that it takes a variable passed to it. **Setsh** will use the value in this variable to set the shape for **t1**. So, when you call **win**, the shape will become a boy or a girl depending on what value is stored in the variable.

#22 Maze III

Assignment

- Add to your Mymaze maze (not the prince/princess maze) at least two moving obstacles. These will be turtles wearing shapes. They could be a fireball (sun) or a spider that you create. We will call them spiders. In your code, make a spider turn 180 degrees every time it hits a maze wall.

- When the **t1** turtle bumps into a spider, the game announces "You lose." Then it resets: the turtle goes back to the start spot with its head up, the same result as when **t1** hits a maze line.

- Put instructions for the user in a text box, something like "Use arrow keys to direct turtle."

Let's work on the first requirement: add two moving obstacles. Make the obstacles turn 180 degrees every time they hit a maze wall.

First you need to create your moving obstacles. To draw a spider shape, double click on one of the empty spots in the Shape Center and then use the drawing tools to make and name your spider shape. Or use a sun or some other ready-made shape. "Hatch" two more turtles (**t3** and **t4**). Go to the Shape Center, click on the shape, and then click on the turtle. This puts the new "clothes" on the turtle so it looks like that shape. Move the turtles around by dragging them with the pointer. Put them at likely spots in your maze.

We will have separate sections of code addressed to each turtle: **t1**, **t3**, and **t4** (**t2** is your destination castle and won't be moving). Here is some pseudocode for example:

> **;talk to t1**
> **;launch a movement for t1**
> **;end that movement under a certain condition.**

For ending the movement, we first used **waituntil**. But when we are talking to multiple turtles all launched into various movements, **waituntil** doesn't work well. There is a similar built-in procedure that we can use. That is **when**.

To jog your memory, look **when** up in the Help vocabulary:

> **when** *true-or-false-instruction-list instruction-list*

> *Starts a parallel process that repeatedly tests whether the first instruction list reports true or false. If it reports true, the second instruction list is run. To stop a **when**, use cancel on the true-or-false-instruction-list, the Cancel menu item, the Stop All menu item, or press Ctrl+Break.*

> *Example:*

> *when [ycor > 50][bk 20]*

In other words, it launches a process that keeps checking the condition in the first set of brackets to see if it is true. When it is true, it runs the instruction inside the second set of brackets.

What's the difference between **when** and **waituntil**? Both **when** and **waituntil** keep checking the condition to see if it is true. When it is true, the **waituntil** procedure simply lets the computer go past it to the next lines of code. It's like **waituntil** is a traffic cop, holding up traffic till the light turns green. When it turns green, the traffic moves on.

When, on the other hand, checks for the green light and then lets the traffic do exactly one thing or one list of things. This might be a little neater for us, with our multiple turtles.

We need to use **when** and some procedures we make to cause the user to either win or lose, depending on whether they meet the winning condition (**t1** touches **t2**), or the losing condition (**t1** touches a red line).

For losing, we will make a **lose** procedure, which uses the **reset** procedure we already made. When the condition is true (**t1** is touching a red line), the computer will run **lose**. **Lose** will announce "You lose!" and then will call **reset.**

For winning, we will use the procedure we already made, **win**. In **win, t1** turns into a cloud and then into something else, waits a bit, and announces "You win!" Then it calls **reset**.

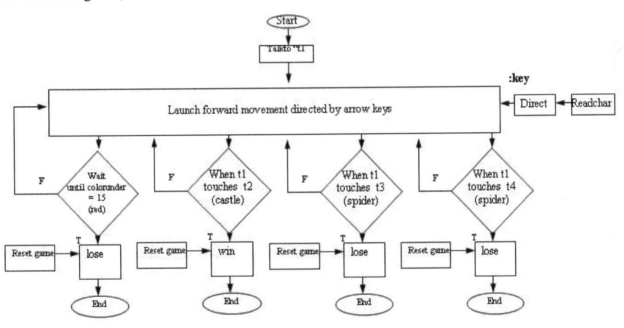

What do you think of the diagram above? Notice that it has four decision-checkers working at once, each represented by a diamond. All are talking to **t1**, because they follow the command to **talkto "t1** at the beginning. Each one leads to an end to the game. Does it represent our program?

I see two problems with it:

1. Where do we launch **t3** and **t4**? They need to be moving back and forth, turning 180 degrees when **colorunder = 15**. Let's put them at the beginning. Our launched movements run at the same time, so we will put them alongside each other.

135

2. For the colorunder check we could use **when** instead of **waituntil**, now that we have changed what happens after **waituntil**. Instead of several commands, now it is just one procedure. Using the same commands (**when**) everywhere would be a little neater, wouldn't it?

Take a look at this diagram now. Will it do?

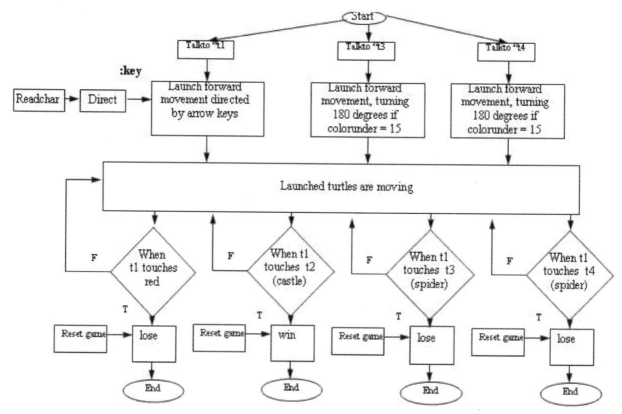

I want you to write some pseudocode in **Main** to match this diagram. DO NOT TURN THE PAGE until you have a draft. It doesn't have to be perfect! Just work on it for a little while, to get the problem into your head.

You're working, right?

Here is my pseudocode:

```
to Main
;talk to t1
;launch forward movement, and turn using arrow keys

;talkto t3
;launch forward movement
;when t3 touches red, turn 180 degrees

;talkto t4
;launch forward movement
;when t4 touches red, turn 180 degrees

;talkto t1

;when t1 touches red, lose (a separate procedure)
;when t1 touches t2, win (a separate procedure)
;when t1 touches t3, lose (a separate procedure)
;when t1 touches t4, lose (a separate procedure)


end
```

Code

Let's recall our Mymaze code from the last lesson:

```
=========
to Main
  talkto "t1
  launch [repeat 2000 [forward 3 direct readchar ] ]
  when [touching? "t1 "t2] [win]
  waituntil [colorunder = 15]
  announce [You lose!]
  reset
end
============
to direct :key
  if (ascii :key) = 28 [seth 270 fd 1]
  if (ascii :key) = 29 [seth 90 fd 1]
  if (ascii :key) = 30 [seth 0 fd 1]
  if (ascii :key) = 31 [seth 180 fd 1]
  if (ascii :key) = 37 [seth 270 fd 1]
  if (ascii :key) = 39 [seth 90 fd 1]
```

138

```
  if (ascii :key) = 38 [seth 0 fd 1]
  if (ascii :key) = 40 [seth 180 fd 1]
  if (:key = "s) [stopall]
end


to go
  Main
end


to win
  announce [You win!]
  talkto "t1
  setsh "cloud wait 2
  setsh random 60 wait 10
  reset
end


to reset
  talkto "t1
  setpos [-319 -164]
  seth 0
  setsh 0
end
```

First of all, let's add a procedure, **to lose**. It will announce "You lose!" and call **reset**. Go ahead and code that one.

Now, let's look at **Main**. We're going to start with our new pseudocode and re-write **Main**. First we'll take the new pseudocode and plug in useful lines of code from the previous Mymaze.

```
to Main
;talk to t1
  talkto "t1
;launch forward movement, and turn using arrow keys
  launch [repeat 2000 [forward 3 direct readchar ] ]
```

Can you come up with code for the next two lines of pseudocode, talking to **t3**? Our forward movement will use **launch, repeat**, and **forward**. Use a large number for the **repeat**.

```
;talkto t3
;launch forward movement
```

Now, code the next line, using **when, colorunder**, and **right**:

```
;when t3 touches red, turn 180 degrees
```

Now, code the next three lines, using the previous three as a model:

> **;talkto t4**
> **;launch forward movement**
> **;when t4 touches red, turn 180 degrees**

Now, code the next line. You will need to **talkto "t1** again. Then you will need **when** and **colorunder**.

> **;when t1 touches red, lose (a separate procedure)**

The next line is already done for us, from the previous Mymaze:

> **;when t1 touches t2, win (a separate procedure)**
> *when [touching? "t1 "t2] [win]*

Now, code the last two lines, using the one above as a model.

> **;when t1 touches t3, lose (a separate procedure)**
> **;when t1 touches t4, lose (a separate procedure)**

> **end**

You'll want to delete the pseudocode lines once you get the thing working. Be sure your maze lines are thick; otherwise the spiders may not see them.

Remember this part of the assignment?

- Put instructions for the user in a text box, something like "Use arrow keys to direct turtle."

Make a text box (using the icon that shows a box filled with "A" or "ABC"). Put in some instructions for the user. Move the box to a good spot by holding down the left mouse button and dragging the box around.

Now, pull it all together and run the maze with the spiders! Save it again as Mymaze.

Extra Credit

Use a slider (a picture of a button that slides) to let the user adjust the speed of the sun/spider. Hatch a slider in MicroWorlds EX using this icon: ⬜. The new slider will be called **slider1**. Use this name instead of a number input, for instance **forward slider1.** It will need to be in the code that launches the movements for the spiders, **t3** and **t4**. Now, adjust the slider and play around with it. Save this as slidermaze, and don't use it for the next lesson!

#23 Maze IV

Assignment

We will enhance Mymaze some more. It now will have three difficulty levels, involving the spiders' speed. We will need one duplicate page for each difficulty level, and also an index page to start from. This will have buttons on it that take us to the easy, medium and difficult pages. We'll also need buttons on those pages to go back to the index page. We will call the index page **Page1** because, in MicroWorlds, any project starts with **Page1** when someone starts playing the game. We want it to start with the index, so we will call that **Page1**.

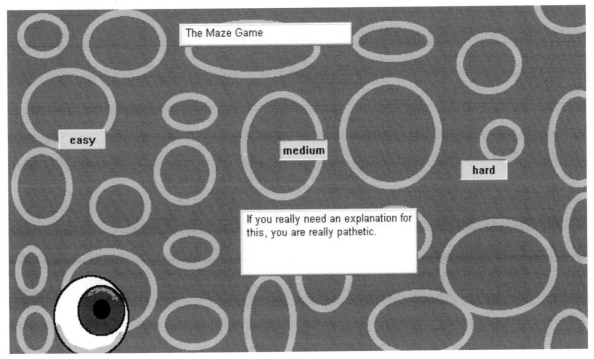

Page1 from Hannah's Maze

Get to Work

We'll be working with multiple pages in our project for this. We need to figure out how to make new pages. Notice that there is a **Pages** menu at the top of the screen. When you click on it, you see you have options to create new pages and to name pages. We will need to do both.

Save your maze under another name for backup, just in case you mess up. Now, in the Mymaze file, create three duplicate pages. To do this, go to the **Pages** menu, and click on **duplicate page**. This makes a new page just like the old one, only this one is called **Page2**. Click **duplicate** two more times. Now you have **Page1, Page2, Page3**, and **Page4**, all the same.

But these names aren't descriptive. Using the Pages menu, go to **Page2**. Then under the Pages menu select **name,** and name the page **easypage**. Go to **Page3** and name it **mediumpage**, and go to **Page4** and name it **hardpage**.

Now you have pages named **Page1, easypage, mediumpage, and hardpage.** These are more than names. They are commands! If you go to the Command Center and type one of the names, that page appears. So we could put the name into our code as a command. We want to call these pages using buttons on the index page, **Page1**.

There are two ways to do this. We could name the button the same as the page. When we push the button, the page comes up. Or we could do it indirectly. Each button could call a procedure we write. The procedure can then call the page name, and can also call a version of **Main** just for that page. Let's do it that way.

Using the Page menu, go to **Page1** and clear the graphics by typing **cg** in the Command Center. Use the scissors icon to get rid of the turtles and the **go** button. Now, using the button creator tool on the left, create three buttons, one named **easy**, one named **medium**, and one named **hard**. Drag them around the page to create a nice arrangement. Decorate the page too.

Now we need to make procedures these buttons will call. On the Procedures Page, make a procedure called **to easy**. It tells the computer what to do when the button called **easy** is pushed.

```
to easy
  easypage
  Maineasy
end
```

You notice that pushing the **easy** button will now call up a version of **Main**, so we won't need any **go** buttons (which used to do that). You can cut them out from all the pages using the scissors icon.

So, what is **Maineasy**? It's a version of **Main** for the **easy** page. You need to create it. Highlight all of your **Main** procedure and hit **control-c** to copy it to the hidden clipboard. Now scroll to another part of your Procedures Page (remember, procedures should be in alphabetical order, except for **Main** first, so this should be near the top!). Hit **control-v** to paste it. Now change the name on the old one to **Maineasy**. Paste another copy. Make the new ones **Mainmedium** and **Mainhard**. We will make changes to make them different from each other in a little while.

We need something else: a way to return from each game page to **Page1**. On each of the game pages, make a button called **index**. To go with it, you'll need to make a procedure for **to index** using this pseudocode:

```
to index
  ;go to Page1
end
```

Put real code in to replace the pseudocode.

Test it. Make adjustments if you need to.

At the moment, you have three different maze pages for your game, with different names but otherwise the same. We need to change the speed of the spiders on each page, in **Maineasy, Mainmedium,** and **Mainhard.** Remember the spiders are **t3** and **t4**. In **Maineasy**, **t3** and **t4** should have the same slow speed. In **Mainmedium**, **t3** and **t4** should both be moving faster. In **Mainhard,** they should be moving even faster. You can shorten the waits to speed things up. Remember, **t1** is moving three turtle steps with every push of the arrow key. So on your easy page, the spiders could be moving three steps and waiting three. On the medium page, they could move three steps and wait two. On the hard page, they could move four steps and wait two, for example. You can make changes in the way the mazes are drawn on the three pages, too.

Now, test your spider speeds. The easy page should be easy, the medium page medium difficulty, and the hard page hard but not impossible. You don't want to lose users because your game is too hard! So adjust the speeds until the reality matches the name for each page. You can make the spiders smaller, too, using the magnifying glass with the minus sign in it.

Exercises

1. Add teleporter booths. Here's how: put a box of another color into the maze. When the **t1** turtle hits the color, it jumps to a different spot in the maze. To find the coordinates of the spot you want to teleport to, move the turtle there using the mouse, and then type **show pos** in the Command Center. OR have the landing spot be a random place in the maze.

2. Create animations using a list of shapes with **setsh** and repeated calls to **forward**.

   a. Have the **t1** turtle animate when it reaches the goal.

   b. Make an animation for the spiders (**t3** and **t4**) as they move, giving realistic motion.

   c. Animate the **t1** turtle as it goes through the maze. One possibility: make it look like Pac-Man. You can make new shapes by double clicking on the blank shapes in the Shapes Center and using drawing tools to construct them.

3. EXTRA CREDIT: a. Create an almost-invisible "ghost spot" that moves around the maze randomly. When the **t1** turtle hits it, **t1** wins the game. b. When someone wins, the bad guys explode.

#24 Get Ready, Get Set for Race

Race is a two-person geography game. Two vehicles are racing in a geographic setting of some kind—the Sahara desert, the moon, Los Angeles, or whatever. To move his vehicle, the player has to answer a question correctly.

We will pull in an image of the setting for the background. Vehicle 1 will go ¼ of the way across the screen every time player 1 correctly answers a question concerning the scene in the background, and the same for vehicle 2 and player 2. The questions alternate between player 1 and player 2. The vehicles can be cars for Los Angeles, or rockets for the Moon, or whatever seems appropriate for other scenes. When someone gets to the finish line, a third turtle which has been hidden shows itself and does a little animation. Of course the object is to get there first!

Construction involves several steps. Today we will do the preparation part.

First, you need a background picture. Select a background from the MicroWorlds 2.0 disk. Or you can pull an image from the Internet. Here's how you do that. We need to find a picture that is free, that is, which the copyright owner has designated as no charge for us to use. You can check out www.picturesfree.org. Or go to www.google.com and set it to safe search. Do this by clicking on "preferences" on the right side, and then choosing SafeSearch Filtering. Choose "use strict filtering." Note—you have to do this every time you re-open your browser; the preference isn't saved for long.

Now that you can safely see Google images, go back to the main Google web page and click on the word "images" just above the blank search line. In the images search, type in "free" and a keyword for what you want to find. If we are looking for the Arizona desert, we could type in "free desert arizona" and see what we get. Once you find a free picture you like, and where the owner has clearly said you can use it free on the Internet (not just your desktop), go to your file menu and use **Save As** to download it to your computer. Save it as a .gif or .bmp. Then open your MicroWorlds file and go to the **File** menu, then **import**. Find the picture file's location and import the picture to your project. If the picture is the wrong size, you will have to re-size it using photo editing software such as Microsoft Picture It. If this sounds like too much trouble, use the drawing tools to draw a background. One student in our class "drew" Antarctica, which is mostly white, with a few ice floes and so on. His racers were penguins. Use your imagination!

Next, create two new turtles using the drawing center and some turtle shape blanks. Give them simple names. They can look like race cars, jackrabbits, eagles, or whatever matches your background. Make them similar but in contrasting colors.

Now, write eight easy questions in a word processor. They should have one- or two-word answers that concern the place you picture. Check your spelling and save. You will copy and paste them into your code shortly.

Finally, consider how you are going to tackle this problem. Make a draft of a flow chart showing the steps you think we'll need. Use a block for a question, and a decision diamond for deciding what to do with the answer. Indicate that this question-answer repeats four times for each user. Show this to your teacher.

#25 Race II

Here are our game specifications:

- The game starts with a **Start** button. It has a thick finish line drawn using the drawing center.

- The game has two users and two turtles. The turtles move a distance to the right (or up) each time the corresponding user answers a question correctly.

- There are four easy questions for each user. After four correct answers, a turtle reaches the finish line.

- If a racing turtle crosses the finish line, a third turtle which has been hidden becomes visible and does an animation of your choice. (This is a procedure called **win**.)

- The racing turtles return to the starting gate when a user presses **Start**. Also, the animated turtle returns to its starting position. (This is a procedure called **setup**.)

One thing to keep in mind as you design your game is that the questions will appear in a large rectangle in the middle of the screen, which will tend to hide the racers if they are also crossing that part of the screen. You can solve this problem by moving the racers to the top or bottom of the screen, or by providing long waits between questions so the user can see where the racer is.

Our flow chart will begin with **Start**, **setup**, and a question block, and then a decision diamond for the answer. If the answer is true, the turtle moves forward. If it is false, we announce "Oops!" and tell the user what the right answer was. In either case, we then go on to the next question. Work again on your sketch of this, and then turn the page to see mine.

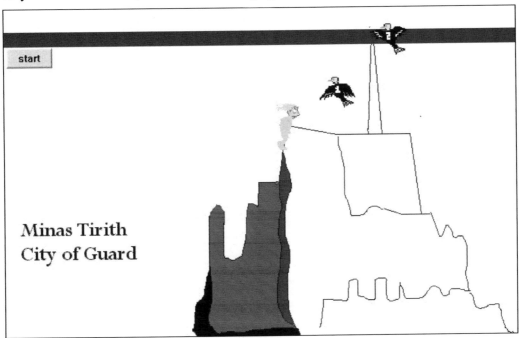

Paul's Race: The Winner! A ghost appears and walks to the top of the mountain.

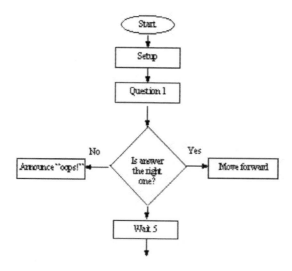

This is a good start for the first question! Now let's add Question 2, just like it.

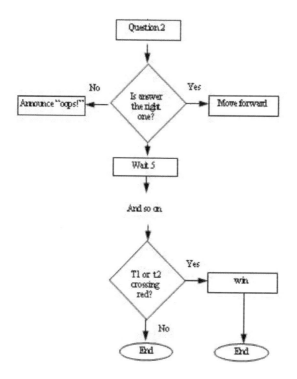

Did your flow chart look a lot like this? I hope so.

Now, we need to translate the flow chart to Logo code for **Main**. For the question, we will use the command **question**. Look it up in the Help vocabulary (see page 22) if you need to.

Next we need to evaluate **answer**, where the user's answer is stored. The flow chart shows a decision diamond with the question, "Is answer the right one?" There are two possible outcomes: right answer and wrong answer. Can you code this? Look up **if** and **ifelse**, to jog your memory. Don't turn the page until you have sketched out some code.

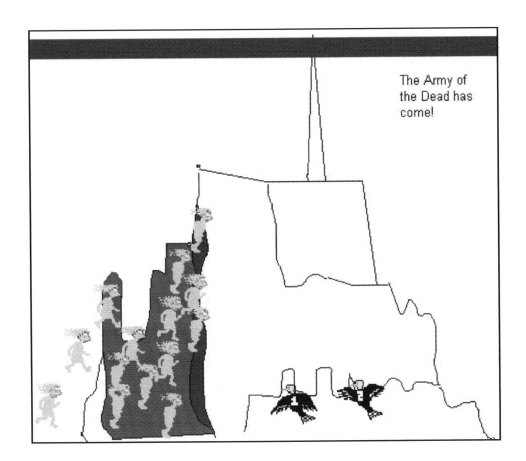

Paul's Race, Page Two (after winning). The army of the dead shows up!

If the user gives the right answer, we can write:

if (answer = "|Mount Vernon|) [talkto "t1 forward 170]

Notice the vertical lines around and quote mark before the two-word answer. If the answer is only one word, you can just use a quote mark before the word, like this:

if (answer = "Vernon) [talkto "t1 forward 170]

Let's work in the other case, where the answer is not equal to Mount Vernon. Can you figure out what to write?

ifelse (answer = "|Mount Vernon|) [talkto "t1 forward 130] [announce [Oops! The right answer was Mount Vernon.]]

For the questions, copy and paste from the list of questions you made already. Address the right user in your question, too, like this:

question [Player 1, What is the name of George Washington's home?]

We also need to make sure the racers can cross the screen all the way to the finish line, if they get the answers all right. Here are two ways to do it:

1. The harder way: using **show pos,** check the coordinates of the start point and the end point. To do this, put **t1** at the start point, go to the Command Center, type **talkto "t1 show pos,** and write down the coordinates. Now move **t1** to the finish line and type **show pos** in the Command Center. Write down those coordinates. The first number is the X coordinate, and the second is the Ycoordinate. You need to subtract the X coordinates for a horizontal race. (X measures horizontal distance across the screen, and Y measures vertical distance.) For instance, your start coordinates might be [-332 -129] and your end coordinates might be [342 -135]. Looking at the first numbers only, your turtle will have to go to the right 332 steps to get to the invisible zero reference line in the middle of the screen. It will have to go another 342 steps to get to the finish line. So the distance traveled is 332 plus 342, or 678 steps. We are asking each turtle four questions to get there, so we divide 678 by 4 to get 169 and a remainder, so we'll round it up to 170. In short, each time we answer a question correctly, we need to go 170 steps. It may be different for yours.

2. If you don't understand what I just did, you can use trial and error to arrive at a step length. Adjust the step length until the turtle lands on the finish line after going forward four times. You can do this in the Command Center—talk to **t1**, put it at the starting place, and tell it to go forward 170, forward 170, and so on four times. Did it land on the line? If not, change the number. Or redraw the line! You can also make the line into a colored rectangle. What's important is that the winner be sitting on the color red = 15 (or other color you choose).

You should have code in place for questions. Test it. Does it work? If not, make adjustments. You can "comment out" the setup line by putting a semicolon in front of it, because it doesn't work yet. Don't forget to remove the semicolon once you actually write the code for **setup.**

148

Now we need to write the code in **Main** that calls **win**, the animation for the winner. In our flow chart there is a decision diamond here. Can you translate that to code? We need to include something else: an instruction to talk to both **t1** and **t2** before we check the color under the turtle. Look in the MicroWorlds Help under **talkto** to see how to address two turtles at once.

Now that you have **Main** written, write **win**. Here are requirements:

- Talk to **t3.**

- Show turtle (**st**) and animate it. Remember to use **setsh** and a list of shapes, then make repeated calls to **forward.**

Now write **setup**. Here are the requirements:

- Talk to **t1**; set its position at the starting gate using **setpos** and the coordinates you got from **show pos** in the Command Center. Set its heading. (Look these up in the Help vocabulary: **setpos** and **seth**.

- Do the same for **t2.**

- Put **t3** at its starting point; this could be on the finish line. Set its heading. Hide **t3** (**ht** is for hide turtle).

Test your code. Does it work? Make adjustments until it does.

Exercise

What if the player doesn't guess four questions right? We need to figure out what to do then. How about announcing "No winners!" Can you figure out where to put that command? Think about it and test your idea.

Crystal's Race: Clifford and T-Bone go for a tiny bone that flips around on winning.

#26 Race III

We're going to add some fun stuff to our game. Let's make a wild set of animations for winning. Here's our next requirement:

- When someone wins, nine turtles appear and run through animations, for example, from a yellow ball to a small ball of fire to a larger ball of fire to a largest ball of fire, and over again.

- Text appears announcing "You won!"

- When the animations are over and the user clicks **Start**, the game resets to original condition.

There's an easy way to take care of the multiple animations and the reset: we'll put the multiple animations on a different page. When someone wins, we go to that page. When someone clicks **Start** again, we go back to **Page1**.

Here's how: Go to **Page1**. Under the **Pages** menu, select **duplicate page.** Now you have another page, **Page2**, that looks just like **Page1**. You can draw on it to make it look somewhat different. You can add some text, such as "You won!!!" Hatch turtles all over the place. Keep track of how many you have. Now, go to the shapes center and make some shapes that go with your theme. You can copy digital pictures and paste them into the turtle shape blocks. Or you can make an explosion. Use the spray can and spray some red and yellow dots. For another shape, make the "explosion" bigger, and for a third, even bigger. You can also make a yellow disk. An animation could cycle through these shapes: disk to small explosion to larger to largest. Or the explosion could start small and get bigger, then repeat. Be sure to name your shapes so you can call them.

Remember how to set up an animation? Install shapes in your Shape Center if you need to. Talk to a particular turtle, set your list of shapes with **setsh**, and then make repeated calls to **forward**. For an animation that isn't really moving, the turtle can move forward by a tiny amount each time, such as 0.01 turtle step (that's one one-hundredth of a turtle step).

Now you need to change **win** so it announces "You win," calls **Page2**, talks to a list of turtles (in brackets), sets shapes, and repeats a command to go forward a tiny amount. Test your new **win** by typing **win** in the Command Center from Page1. Does it work?

Now be sure to adjust **setup** so that it goes back to **Page1** to start the game over.

One more thing: the users need some directions. On **Page1** you can add a text box that says something like "This is a two-player racing game. Answer questions to win!"

Play your game! Use the Presentation Mode under the Gadgets menu. (To get out of Presentation Mode, click on the black surrounding area.)

#27 Hangman I: Going Loopy

Now we are going to learn how to make loops. A loop repeats the same set of steps over and over, until an ending condition is met. Loops are common to all computer languages, and it's time we learned about them! We'll need to know about loops for this game, Hangman. This is a game that

- asks a user for a letter, and

- evaluates it to see if it is one of the letters we had chosen.

Then it does those again and again, until the user has guessed six wrong answers. That's a loop, all right!

Here is a flow chart of a simple loop:

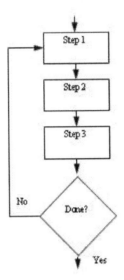

Notice the steps that follow each other down the page. Then comes the decision diamond. If we are done, we go on. If we are not done, we go back to Step 1.

We've actually used loops before: **repeat** is a simple loop, for example. We could say

repeat 6 [lots of steps]

That would be a loop that repeats six times. We could use **repeat** and end the Hangman loop when the user has guessed six times. But that won't do—we need to end the loop when the user has guessed six *wrong* answers. We have some more to learn.

Our loop needs to count only the wrong guesses, stopping the loop at six. We will need what is called a *counter* in our loop. A counter is another universal element in computer languages. We create a variable called **counter** and set its value to 0. We go through the series of steps, and at the end of the series we add 1 to what's in the variable **counter**. Then we go through the series of steps again, and add 1 to the counter again. When the counter equals six, we stop. This is called an **incremented loop**. (Incrementing is going step-by-step.) There are various ways to set one up in Logo.

151

In most computer languages, the code for incrementing at the end of the loop looks something like this:

:counter = :counter + 1

If you have had any algebra, you might think this means something like

x = x + 1

Here, x is a math variable that stands for any number. If you substitute 10 for x, you get 10 equals 10 plus 1. We all know that's silly! But in computer languages statements like that are common. Can you figure out why?

It's because of the nature of computer variables—they are nothing more than storage places. So you look at the right-hand side of the statement first. You take the value stored in **counter**, add one to it, and put the number back into storage. It's really not that strange after all. Let's take a look at that line again:

:counter = :counter + 1

It means this: Add 1 to the value in **counter**, and then store it again in the storage spot called **counter**.

Now, Logo has some quirks, and here is one! That line of code won't work. We have to use this line of code instead:

make "counter sum :counter 1

I hope you can see that it means the same thing. Let's draw a picture of a loop with a counter:

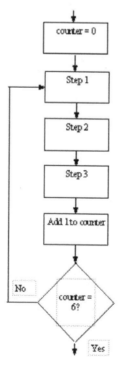

Let's make some test code. Open a new file and type this into your Procedures Page:

```
to Main
  local "counter
  make "counter 0
  talkto "t1
  forward 15 wait 1 ;step 1
  right 90  ;step 2
  forward 15 wait 1 ;step 3
  make "counter sum :counter 1
end

to Start
  Main
end
```

Now, go to the Graphics Page and make a **Start** button. What do you think will happen when we push it? Go ahead and do it.

I hope you weren't expecting a loop, because we didn't make one! Our code just follows a sequence of steps and then ends. We need to make an adjustment to get it to loop.

Our loop has to have some code to make it go back, and also an exit condition. Let's work on the go-back part first. Go to the Help vocabulary and type in **loop**. What do you see? Nothing! We need another idea. How about using **launch**? That starts up a process that keeps repeating itself until we stop it. That sounds like the definition of a loop!

Here's what the Help vocabulary says about **launch**:

> *launch word-or-list-to-run*
>
> *Runs the input as an independent parallel process. If the process is launched from the Command Center, the cursor reappears immediately. Use **cancel**, the Cancel menu item, the Stop All menu item, or Ctrl+Break to stop the process. See also **forever**.*

Let's look up **forever**, too:

> *forever word-or-list-to-run*
>
> *Runs the input repeatedly as an independent parallel process. Use cancel, the Cancel menu item, the Stop All menu item, or Ctrl+Break to stop the process. See also launch.*

Let's test **launch**. We'll set up our loop inside a set of brackets following **launch**. Change your **Main** code to look like this:

```
============
to Main
  local "counter
  make "counter 0
  launch
  [
    talkto "t1
    forward 15 wait 1
    right 90
    forward 15 wait 1
    make "counter sum :counter 1
  ]
end
============
to Start
  Main
end
```

Now, before we dive into an endless loop, we have to plan for a way to get out. Make a button called **stopall,** which will stop all processes. That way we can stop the action.

Go to **Page1** and push **Start.** What happens? My turtle only takes a couple of steps! Remember that when we have used **launch** before, we have included a repeat, so the code said **launch [repeat 2000[some steps]].** So we could put in **repeat 2000,** and another set of brackets.

Maybe we could use **forever** instead. Replace the word **launch** with **forever** in your **Main** code. What happens? My turtle starts making boxes and boxes! I have to press the **stopall** button to stop him. That is just what I want.

Now we have an endless loop with an exit condition, the **stopall** button. But our exit condition has nothing to do with our counter. How can we change that?

Here's an important troubleshooting idea. Let's add a marker to see what part of the program is executing. We'll add a line that say **show :counter.** When a number is printed in the Command Center, we will know that the program got as far as our marker. Add a line of code inside the loop that says **show :counter,** like this:

```
to Main
  local "counter
  make "counter 0
  forever
  [
    talkto "t1
    forward 15 wait 1
    right 90
    forward 15 wait 1
    show :counter
```

```
        make "counter sum :counter 1
    ]
  end
```

Now, test it. Does a series of numbers appear in the Command Center? If not, go back and check your code against mine.

How can we stop this loop using the counter? Let's add a **when** process that looks for the number 6. To jog our memories, let's look up **when** in the Help vocabulary.

> **when** *[true-or-false-instruction-list] [instruction-list]*
>
> *Starts a parallel process that repeatedly tests whether the first instruction list reports true or false. If it reports true, the second instruction list is run. To stop a **when**, use cancel (only on the true-or-false-instruction-list), the Cancel menu item, the Stop All menu item, or press Ctrl+Break.*

We could use **when** to continually check for the exit condition, counter equal to 6. Or we could use **if** to check once each time we go through the loop. Let's try both.

Make a **when** line that says when *what's in* the counter equals 6, **stopall**. (**Stopall** means stop all processes.) Where should we put it? Since it is the exit condition, let's put it just inside the loop, at the end:

```
    to Main
      local "counter
      make "counter 0

      forever
      [
        talkto "t1
        forward 15 wait 1
        right 90
        forward 15 wait 1
        show :counter
        make "counter sum :counter 1
        when [:counter = 6][stopall]
      ]
    end

    to Start
      Main
    end
```

Now, test it. Does it stop when the counter gets to 6, or do you have to press the **stopall** button?

Now, replace the **when** line with an **if** line, like this:

```
    if (:counter = 6) [stopall]
```

155

Remember that **if** uses parentheses instead of brackets on the condition it is checking.

Does that work too?

Exercises

1. Start with a new MicroWorlds file. Make a program separate from our example, without looking at it. This program uses **forever** to set up a two- or three-step loop. Have your turtle with pen down jump "up" and then come back down to a different spot. Use a **stopall** button to get out of the loop.

2. Create a new variable, **counter**, for this program. Set its value to 0 before the loop starts. Inside the loop, add one to the counter. Also inside the loop, add code to show the counter in the Command Center. Check to see if it works.

3. Now, hatch two new turtles on **Page1**. If the counter's value is 10, **talkto** t2 and animate it as a snake (or some other critter) to wriggle to the left across the screen. If the counter's value is 20, **talkto** t3 and animate it as a bee (or some other critter) to fly to the right. If its value is 30, **stopall**.

4. Now, replace the **if** statements with **when** statements. Do they work? Do you know why or why not? Remember that **when** continually checks for the same thing.

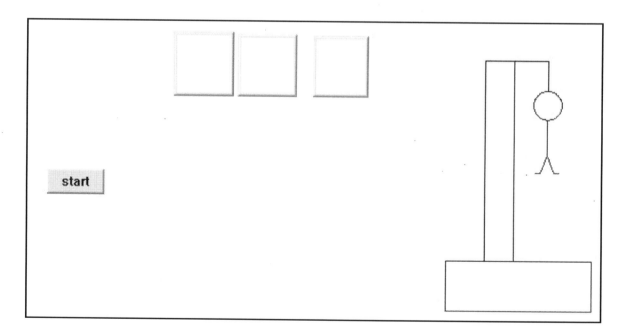

Nicole's Hangman

#28 Hangman II

(The rest of the Hangman lessons may be more advanced than a middle-school student would like. If so, please feel free to skip them and go on to the next game, City.)

Now, how can we apply what we have learned to Hangman?

In Hangman, the user has six tries to guess the letters in a word. When a guess is wrong, the computer draws a piece of a hanging man. After six wrong guesses, the man is a goner.

We'll leave the drawing part till later. For now, we'll just count the wrong guesses. Let's translate this into some requirements for our first, simplified version:

- Setup: Choose a word of three or four letters for the user to guess. Set up the right number of text boxes, one for each letter in the word.

- The computer will ask the user to guess a letter.

- The computer will compare each guess to the letters chosen.

- If the letter is one of those chosen, the computer will print it in the right text box.

- If the letter is incorrect, the computer will count the wrong guess

- The computer will repeat the series of steps, beginning with asking the user to guess a letter.

- After six wrong guesses, the loop ends.

We need to replace the steps in the loop that move the turtle with steps that have to do with Hangman.

Setup

First, let's set up our Graphics Page in a new MicroWorlds file. We will set up three small text boxes on the screen to hold each letter when it is guessed. We will use the **print** command to put the letter into the text box rather than into the Command Center.

To make a text box, go to the A or ABC icon. Click on it, then on the graphics screen. Draw a good-sized text box, at least one inch square. It tells you that its name is **text1**. Now, using your right-hand mouse button, right-click on the text box. A screen pops up. In MicroWorlds EX, choose "edit," and you see a box that says "Show Name" is checked. In MicroWorlds 2.0, you don't have to choose "edit" first; you just see the box. Click next to "Show Name" to uncheck it, and click "OK." Now the name **text1** is hidden.

Make a **Start** button. On the Procedures Page, write a procedure for **Start**.

Plan the Code

Our loop will be modeled after the loop we did in the last lesson. But our steps will be different. Instead of moving the turtle, the steps will do something else. Let's paste in that code from your other file for starters, and replace the three steps with Step 1, Step 2, and Step 3. We can put a comment mark in front of Step 1, Step 2, and Step 3 to remind us that they don't really work. It should look like this:

```
to Main
  local "counter
  make "counter 0

  forever
  [
    talkto "t1
    ;Step 1
    ;Step 2
    ;Step 3
    show :counter
    make "counter sum :counter 1
    if (:counter = 6)[stopall]
  ]
end
```

What will the first step be for Hangman? Here are the loop requirements again:

- The computer will ask the user to guess a letter.

- The computer will compare each guess to the letters chosen.

- If the letter is one of those chosen, the computer will print it in the right text box.

- If the letter is incorrect, the computer will count the wrong guess.

It looks like the first step inside the loop will be one asking the user to guess a letter.

Can you make a sketch of a diagram of our Hangman loop? Write the diagram instructions in pseudocode for now. Don't turn the page until you do.

You're working, right?

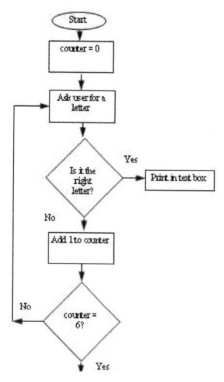

Here's a sketch to start with. You see that inside the loop the program asks for a letter and then evaluates it. If it is the right letter, it prints it in a text box. If it isn't, it adds one to the counter and goes back to the beginning of the loop, asking for a letter again.

Let's choose DOG for our hidden word. From our diagram, here is some pseudocode for the loop steps:

> **;ask the user for a letter**
> **;if the answer is a d, print it in a text box**
> **;if the answer is an o, print it in a text box**
> **;if the answer is a g, print it in a text box**
> **;otherwise, add one to the counter**
> **;if the counter = 6, stop the loop.**

Sandboxing

Now, we need to do some sandboxing.

What tools do we need? We want to ask for a letter from the user, test it, and print it in the text box.

Remember **question**? Look it up in the Help vocabulary (see page 22 if you forgot how). Look up **answer**, too. Now, look up **print,** to jog your memory.

If we just tell the computer to **print** the letter and have only one text box, the letters might end up out of order. That's why we need three different little text boxes. We'll tell the computer to put a **d** in **text1**, an **o** in **text2**, or a **g** in **text3**. Here's how we differentiate: we **talkto** the text boxes, the way we **talkto** turtles. So we **talkto "text1**, and so on.

Come up with some Logo code for the steps inside the loop. Type your loop steps into **Main**, replacing Step 1, Step 2, and Step 3. Work on it for a while before you turn the page and look at my code.

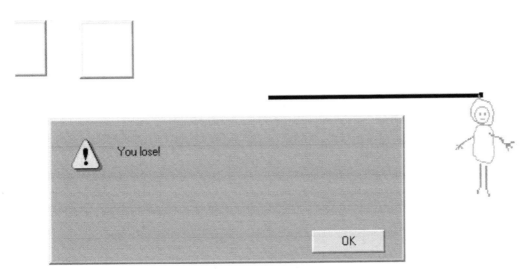

My Hangman

After you click "OK," eyes close.

Here is mine:

```
to Main
  local "counter
  make "counter 0

  forever
  [
  question [Please give me a letter]
  if (answer = "d) [talkto "text1 print answer]
  if (answer = "o) [talkto "text2 print answer]
  if (answer = "g) [talkto "text3 print answer]
  show :counter
  make "counter sum :counter 1
  if (:counter = 6)[stopall]
  ]
end

to Start
  Main
end
```

Test your creation.

Hmm, mine is counting all the answers, not just the wrong ones! I forgot to put something in to account for "otherwise" add one to the counter. Hmm. We need to change our line that adds one to the counter, using this logic:

> ;if it's not d, o , or g, add one to the counter.

Back to the Sandbox for Some Logic!

We need to construct a statement that means "it's not d, o, or g," that will be either true or false. So we need to look at these logical operators: **and**, **not**, and **or**.

Let's consider this Boolean statement (statement that is either true or false):

> **It is raining.**

Let's use it like this:

> **If (it is raining) [take my umbrella].**

If the Boolean statement in parentheses evaluates to true, then we take the action that follows. If it evaluates to false, we don't.

162

How about this?

If (it is raining) and (I have to go out)[take the umbrella].

Now the **and** is linking two Boolean statements. If *both* Boolean statements are true, then the compound statement is true, and we take the action following. Sounds kind of obvious, doesn't it?

What if I replaced **and** with **or**? Then only one of the Boolean statements, or conditions, needs to be true for the compound statement to evaluate to true, so we take the following action.

If (it is raining) or (I have to go out)[take the umbrella].

We can see that **or** isn't the right operator to use here. It doesn't make sense. But we could use **or** in a different sentence.

If (it is raining) or (the weatherman says it will rain) [take the umbrella].

Here if either of these conditions is true, the compound statement is true, and so we take the following action. That is the nature of the **or** operator: only one of the conditions has to be true.

Let's go over that again. Is this compound statement true or false?

(it is raining) and (I have to go out)

It's true if both of the conditions in parentheses are true, and otherwise it is false.

Using **or**,

(it is raining) or (I have to go out)

the linked statement is true if one of the conditions in parentheses is true.

Why are we so interested in whether it evaluates to true or false? Because when we use **when** and **if**, in Logo, we have to have a condition that evaluates to true or false. Specifically, we want a condition that looks something like this:

If (answer = "d or answer = "o or answer = "g) [add one to the counter]

Oops! In this case, if one of those small statements is true, we add one to the counter. That's not what we want at all! We want to add one to the counter if the answer is NOT d, o, or g! What do we do?

There's another logical operator called **not**. It simply changes a condition's true evaluation to false, and vice versa. So what we really want is this:

If not (answer = "d or answer = "o or answer = "g) [add one to the counter]

You may think this logic is pretty strange. It's like speaking English, kind of. But you have to use your logical brain powers to make sense of it. Don't pooh-pooh it though! Logic is very important for programmers. This logic stuff is just the way computers think!

Now, back to the line above. Of course, I am writing in pseudocode, so it isn't really Logo yet. How are we going to translate it to Logo?

Here's what Help says about **not**:

> ***not***
>
> ***not*** *true-or-false*
>
> *Reports the logical inverse of its input. See **and** and **or**.*
>
> *Example:*
>
> *show empty? [ ]*
>
> *true*
>
> *show not empty? [ ]*
>
> *false*

In other words, the input for **not** is a condition that evaluates to true or false, and no parentheses are needed. It's pretty much like *not* in English.

But **or** isn't like *or* in English. Here's what help says about **or**:

> ***or***
>
> ***or*** *true-or-false1 true-or-false2*
>
> **(*or*** *true-or-false1 true-or-false2 true-or-false3...)*
>
> *Reports true if any of its inputs report true. If more than two inputs are used, **or** and its inputs must be enclosed in parentheses. See **and** and **not**.*
>
> *Examples:*
>
> *show or (2 = 2) (3 = 5)*
>
> *true*
>
> *show (or (2 = 2) (3 = 5) (8 = 9))*
>
> *true*

In other words, since we have three inputs concerning d, o, and g, we need to use parentheses as in the second example. Here is our rough code again:

If not (answer = "d or answer = "o or answer = "g) [add one to the counter]

Let's use **or** properly **(or ...)** and see what happens:

If not (or answer = "d answer = "o answer = "g) [add one to the counter]

One more thing we have to do: change the last part to Logo.

make "counter sum :counter 1

Put this line in your code and see what happens!

If not (or answer = "d answer = "o answer = "g) [make "counter sum :counter 1]

Does it count only the wrong answers now? It should.

Exercises

Tell whether these compound statements are true or false:

1. Dogs like walks **and** trees can swim.

2. Dogs like walks **or** trees can swim.

3. Not (dogs like walks **and** trees can swim).

4. Not (dogs like walks **or** trees can swim).

#29 Hangman III

Here's a recap of the requirements we have covered so far in our Hangman game:

- Setup: Choose a word of three or four letters for the user to guess. Set up the right number of text boxes, one for each letter in the word.

- The computer will ask the user to guess a letter.

- The computer will compare each guess to the letters chosen.

- If the letter is one of those chosen, the computer will print it in the right text box.

- If the letter is incorrect, the computer will count the wrong guess

- The computer will repeat the series of steps, beginning with asking the user to guess a letter.

- After six wrong guesses, the loop ends.

Here's another set of requirements for us to take up now:

- After six wrong guesses, the computer announces "You lose! The word was _____." The game ends.

- If the user guesses all the letters correctly, the computer announces "You win!" and ends the game.

First, let's make a diagram of our game with these two exit conditions.

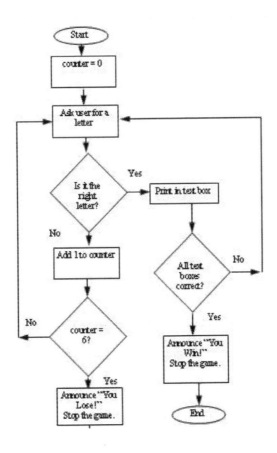

You see that I have drawn the two exit conditions (losing and winning) as parallel, independent processes. That's why there are two separate paths coming down the page. We will work on the "you lose" path first.

First, we need to come up with a line of code that does what the "announce you lose" diagram box says. Think about it and write it down on scratch paper. You will need to use **announce** and **stopall**.

Now, we need to figure out where to put the new line of code. Here is our Main from the last lesson:

```
to Main
  local "counter
  make "counter 0
  forever
  [
    question [Please give me a letter]
    if (answer = "d) [talkto "text1 print answer]
    if (answer = "o) [talkto "text2 print answer]
    if (answer = "g) [talkto "text3 print answer]
    show :counter
    if not ( or answer = "d answer = "o answer = "g) [make "counter sum :counter 1]
    if (:counter = 6)[stopall]
  ]
end
```

Do you see the line we need to change? It's this one:

if (:counter = 6)[stopall]

Let's change it to this:

if (:counter = 6)[announce [You lose!] stopall]

Does that work? It should. Or sort of, anyway. Now my game is telling me that I lost even though I guessed the right answers! What I need is the other exit condition operating.

Let's look at the diagram again for that one. It says, in pseudocode,

;if all text boxes are correct, announce you win, and stop the game.

Let's go ahead and insert that pseudocode, just inside the loop at the end.

How could the computer tell if all the boxes are correctly filled? What ideas do you have? Think about it for a minute.

Here's one way: we could create variables to hold the correct responses, and fill them as we fill the text boxes. Then we could check the variables to see if their contents are correct. Then we would stop the loop. (There's another way that involves using the text boxes as sort-of variables, with their own odd set of commands, but that doesn't transfer to other languages very well so we won't use it.)

We can create the shadow variables in the same line where we created **counter**. How about this:

local [counter letter1 letter2 letter3]

If the answer is **d**, we want to print the **d** in the text box and *also* put the **d** in the variable **letter1**. If the answer is **o**, we want to print the **o** in the text box and *also* put the **o** in the variable **letter2**. Same with **g**, for **letter3**. Can you see how to do this? Try it yourself and see if it works. Then turn the page to see mine.

I changed loop steps to look like this:

```
to Main
  local [counter letter1 letter2 letter3]
  make "counter 0
  forever
  [
     question [Please give me a letter]
     if (answer = "d) [talkto "text1 print answer make "letter1 answer]
     if (answer = "o) [talkto "text2 print answer make "letter2 answer]
     if (answer = "g) [talkto "text3 print answer make "letter3 answer]
     show :counter
     if not ( or answer = "d answer = "o answer = "g) [make "counter sum :counter 1]
     if (:counter = 6)[announce [You lose!] stopall]
     ;if all text boxes are correct, announce you win, and stop the game.
  ]
end
```

Now that the variables are filling up nicely, how do we check that the contents are correct? Let's use this simple line of reasoning. If **letter1** contains **d** and **letter2** contains **o** and **letter3** contains **g**, then announce "You win" and stop the game. The key word here is **and**. Remember its special use from the lesson on logic? I will jog your memory.

> **If (it is raining) and (I have to go out)[take the umbrella].**

Now the **and** is linking two Boolean statements. If *both* Boolean statements are true, then we take the action following.

What if I use **or**? Then only one of the Boolean statements needs to be true.

> **If (it is raining) or (the weatherman says it will rain) [take the umbrella].**

Let's go back to our hangman problem.

We want to say

> **;if all text boxes are correct, announce you win, and stop the game.**

Actually, we want to use the variable names letter1, letter2, and letter3 to say something more like this:

> **;if ([letter1 contains d] and [letter2 contains o] and [letter3 contains g])**
> **[announce you win and stop the game]**

First, let's look first at the simple statements. How will we translate [letter1 contains d] to Logo?

The equals sign is a Boolean (true-false) operator in Logo. A statement using = is a Boolean statement, evaluating to true or false. So let's try using =, with a space before and after. Will this work?

169

letter1 = d

We need say "what's in" letter1, not the name of the variable, so we will use the dots operator :

:letter1 = d

But the computer probably will try to read **d** as a procedure or action, not as a name, so we had better put quotes in front of it. Let's try

:letter1 = "d

We should be able to construct the simple statements from that example. Now, let's look up **and** again in the MicroWorlds Help.

> *and*
>
> *and true-or-false1 true-or-false2*
>
> *(and true-or-false1 true-or-false2 true-or-false3...)*
>
> *Reports true if all its inputs report true. If more than two inputs are used, **and** and its inputs must be enclosed in parentheses. See **or** and **not**.*
>
> *Example:*
>
> *show (and 2 = 2 5 = 5 6 = 6)*
>
> *true*

We can see that **and**, like other MicroWorlds procedures, is followed by its inputs, separated by spaces. If there are more than two inputs, we need to enclose **and** with the inputs in parentheses.

Now, let's see if you can use this information to cast this pseudocode into Logo:

;if ([letter1 contains d] and [letter2 contains o] and [letter3 contains g])[announce you win and stop the game]

Work on it and test it.

Exercises

1. Make a **reset** procedure that is called at the beginning of the game, so that the user can play the game again and again and have the text boxes cleared by pressing **Start** to start the game. Look up **cleartext** in the Help vocabulary and use it.

2. Change the guessed word to a longer word with different letters. Remember to use **copy** and **paste**, and then make changes, to reduce the amount you have to retype.

3. Extra credit: Consider this problem: Create code that rejects the "right" letters if they are used more than once. How would you solve it? Create pseudocode for key lines. Cast into Logo.

#30 Hangman IV

Here's our next requirement:

Make a six-piece drawing that adds a piece of a hanging man each time the user makes a wrong guess. Use hidden turtles for each piece of the man (**ht** is a command that hides a turtle; **st** is a command that shows a hidden turtle.)

First, go to the shape center and make six shapes that will make up a hanging man. You can name them like this: noose, head, body, arm1, arm2, legs.

Now, on your Page1, use the drawing tools to draw a bar that the noose will hang from. Hatch five more turtles. Put the shapes on them in order: noose on **t1**, head on **t2**, body on **t3**, and so on. Drag them around so that they make a drawing of a hanging man. Change the part drawings if you need to make them match up. Be sure to put the hanging man drawing off to the side of the page, where it won't be covered by the question/announcement box in the middle.

From Hannah's Hangman: Hanging in Progress

What we want to do is at the beginning hide the turtles that make up the drawing, and show them one by one as the counter number increases. Can you think of a way to do that? Think about it before you turn the page. Use **ht** to hide a turtle and **st** to show a turtle.

171

Here's what we can do: At the beginning of the code, just after the list of variables, talk to a list of all the turtles, and then command **ht** for hide turtle.

Lower down in the program, inside the loop near the end, we will make a set of **if** statements, meaning:

;if the counter equals 1, talk to t1, show the turtle, and set its shape to noose.

Can you translate that to Logo? And make more for the rest of the body parts?

Exercises

1. Make another shape that shows the hanging man is a goner (eyes are x's for instance). Change to that shape after the computer announces "You lose!"

2. Make a separate procedure called **win**. In the winning case, hide all but one of the turtles. For the one still showing, change the shape to something fun, like a fireball. Animate it.

Hannah's Hangman Is a Goner!

#31 City I

This is a game that asks the user for directions and then draws a busy street, lined with houses and full of animated characters zipping back and forth. Or it could be a variation on this; one student drew an army camp of barracks with jeeps, trucks, and airplanes moving through and above it, complete with blinking lights. Use your imagination when you plan your city! Here are two examples:

My City

Paul's Army Camp

173

Here is the plan:

- The user presses the **Start** button.

- The drawing turtle moves to the left edge of the screen, near the bottom so the question boxes won't cover up the houses it draws.

- The computer says to the user, "I will build you a house. Do you want big or small? (type big or small)"

- The turtle, **t1**, draws a house, sized either big or small. The houses are identical except for size.

- It waits a bit so the user can see the drawing.

- The computer asks, "Do you want 1 or 2 windows?"

- T1 draws one or two windows. It waits a bit.

- The computer asks, "Do you want a red or blue house?"

- T1 colors the house in with red or blue (or two other colors you choose). Now the house is built. It moves to the right some steps.

- The computer asks, "Do you want another house? Y or N"

- If the user answers "Y," the loop starts over. We could end up with a street lined with houses.

- After the city is drawn, the program launches at least three animations walking or flying down the street (across the screen).

- The user can stop the animations and start over by pressing **Start**.

There are two things about this program I want you to notice right off the bat. One is that it contains a loop. It repeats a set of steps over and over. The other is that it uses variables. The **house** procedure will use a variable sent from **Main** to determine what size to draw the house.

I want you to take out a pencil and paper and work on a flow chart for this program. Don't turn the page to look at mine until you have worked on it for 10 minutes. Hint: it looks a lot like the one for Race, but there is a loop in it.

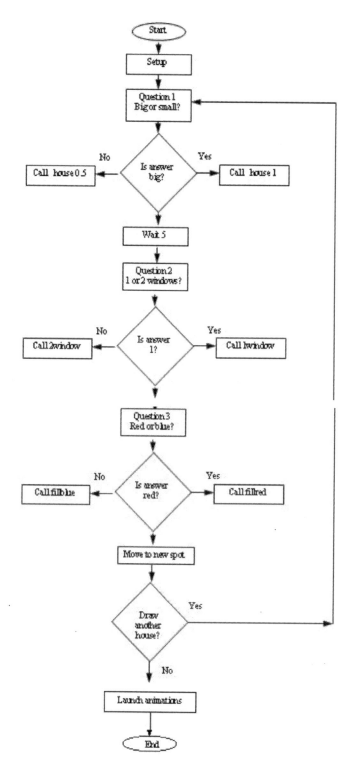

Flow Chart for City

First, let's consider what code we will use to make our loop. We will have a bunch of steps, and at the end of the steps, we will get input from the user on whether to loop or not. We could pattern our loop after our Hangman loop, using **forever** to start it, and stopping it with an **if** statement at the end. For example, we can ask the user if he wants to continue, Y or N.

;if the answer is N, animate, wait a while, and stop the action.

Notice that that is not Logo, but pseudocode, so we put a semicolon in front of it.

Here's another way to do it: don't use **forever** at the top; just start the steps in the loop. Then at the end of the loop, ask the user if he or she wants to continue, Y or N. If the answer is Y, we call **Main**. If it is N, we don't. So we are calling **Main** from within **Main**. Sound strange? It works, as long as you have a way to get out of the loop. The problem here is that the first line of our Main is **setup**, but we don't want to run **setup** every time we go through the loop. We would have to move **setup** out of **Main** and into the **Start** button procedure. So **Start** would look like this:

> **to Start**
>   **cg**
>   **setup**
>   **Main**
> **end**

The advantage of this plan is that we don't have to stop all the action to get out of the loop. So the animations can just keep chugging along until the user presses the **Start** button or closes the window. We could add a **stopall** button too.

So, which loop shall we use? Let's use the one that calls **Main** from **Main**. We could use practice with that one. Now our flow chart for **Main** looks a little different at the top:

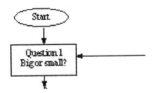

Next, let's brush up on variables a little. Remember that variables are storage places, like pigeonhole mailboxes. A first line for a procedure can create a variable storage place, like this:

> **to house :size**

Here **house** is the name of the procedure, and **size** is the name of the variable used inside the procedure. So, now the procedure **house** needs one input. When we call this procedure **house** from **Main**, we need to send it an input to go into the variable **size**. So our command from **Main** would look like this:

> **house 1**

for the full-sized house, or

> **house 0.5**

for the half-sized house. Now, inside the procedure **house**, we will use this number that **Main** sent over. Instead of **forward 1**, we can say **forward :size**. This means "go forward by what's in **size**." We're reading those two dots in front of **size** as "what's in." We will worry about the details of **house** in a minute.

Now, using the flowchart, code your **Main** procedure. Use **question**, **answer**, and **if** statements. Brush up on those by looking at the Help vocabulary if you need to. Remember to create the loop by calling **Main** at the end, like this:

> **ifelse (answer = "y)[Main][animate]**

In the middle of **Main** we need a line that moves the turtle to a new spot to draw a new house. Let's consider that line. First pick the pen up. Then we need to drop the turtle down from the windowsill to the street level, and then move it to the right. To drop it to street level, you could make use of the built-in procedure **sety**. If you command **sety –120**, the turtle will drop up or down from wherever it is, to the level of Y= -120. Try it: type **sety –120** in the Command Center, and see where your turtle goes. If this isn't where your street level is, put the turtle at your street level and type **show pos** in the Command Center. It will give you two numbers, the x and y coordinates. Take the second one; that's your y coordinate. Now test **sety** with that number. After dropping the turtle to street level, move it to the right 100 or 125 turtle steps. Add a comment to remind you what is going on, like this: **;moving the turtle to a new spot.**

To get our program going, we need to code these procedures: **setup, house** with one input, **1window, 2window, fillred, fillblue,** and **animate**. I already gave you **Start**.

To code **setup**, put your turtle where you want it to start, using the mouse. This will be along the left side of the Graphics Page, fairly low. Now use **show pos** in the Command Center to find its coordinates. In the **setup** procedure, tell **t1** to set its position there.

How do we code **house**? This is actually from *Computer Science Pure and Simple Book 1*, where we drew a house and then added a variable that re-sized it. First, don't worry now about the variable use inside the procedure. Make a procedure **to house :size** that draws a house but doesn't actually use **size** yet. It can be a simple house, or a more complex one. A simple house is a square 50 turtle steps on a side, a triangle on top of it, and a door. Remember that if the turtle is drawing a triangle with equal sides, it turns 120 degrees at each corner.

Next we will make two window procedures, **1window** and **2window.** One draws one window, one draws two. Each one starts from the spot where the drawing of **house** ended. Make a little sketch with dimensions on it, to tell your turtle where to go to start a window.

Next, we will make two procedures, **fillred** and **fillblue**. In each one, the turtle picks its pen up (**pu**) and then takes a step or two into the square that represents the side of the house. It sets the color in the bucket using **setc**; for example, **setc 15** sets it to red, and **setc 105** sets it to blue. It puts its pen down (**pd**). Then it fills the side of the house with color using **fill**.

Animate is a fancy procedure we will develop later. For the time being, just make a dummy:

> **to animate**
> **end**

This will show us if our program as a whole works.

Make a **Start** button.

So, at the moment, we have a program that loops using a call to **Main** at the end of the loop. It draws houses that are the same size, with different colors, with different numbers of windows. The animation planned for the end isn't in place yet, and neither is the house re-size. Test it and tinker with it until it works!

Exercise

After you get the simplified program to work using the call to **Main** at the end of the loop (called a recursive call to **Main**), save your work. Now save it again in a different file, and see if you can get the program to loop using **forever**. Put **forever** at the top of the series of steps in **Main**, with brackets [and] around the steps. You will need to change two more things to provide a way to stop the loop. These are the line at the end of the loop that begins with **if** and provides a way out of the loop, and the procedure **animate**. You will need to put the command **stopall** inside the animate procedure. If you find your program stuck in an infinite loop, press **control-alt-delete** keys at the same time to bring up a menu that allows you to shut down the MicroWorlds application and try again. After you play with it, put this exercise aside; it isn't the program we will move forward with in the next lesson.

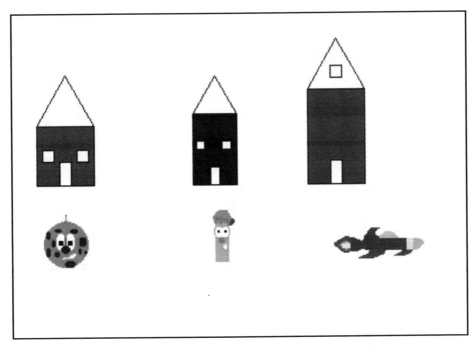

Stephen's City. The Veggie Tales characters animate.

179

#32 City II

We are moving forward with the version of **Main** from the last lesson in which **Main** calls itself in order to create a loop. In order to finish our program, we need to flesh out the two procedures **house** and **animate**. In this lesson we will work on **house**.

Here is our requirement: add a variable to **house**, and change the line in **Main** that calls **house** to add a variable input.

We need to re-size **house**. First, let's jog our memories again on what we learned about variables. Remember that a variable for a computer is a storage spot, like one of a lot of cubbyholes or mailboxes set up in the computer's RAM, or temporary memory. We have created a variable named **size** in our house procedure. We are going to take the user's input, *big* or *small*. If it's *big*, we will send the number 1 over from **Main** as the input to **house** to be stored in **size**. If it's *small*, we'll send over the number 0.5. Here's what the sending looks like:

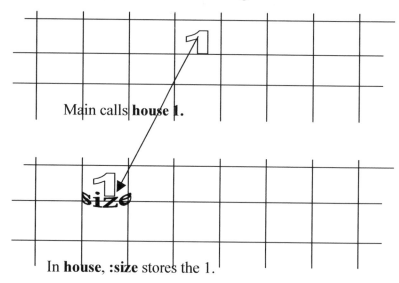

Main calls **house** 1.

In **house**, :size stores the 1.

So, inside of our **house** procedure, what do we do with what's in this variable **size**? We are going to multiply all the lengths in the house drawing by it. So if **size** contains 1, we get a house 50 turtle steps wide. If it contains 0.5, we get one that is 25 turtle steps wide.

In your **house** procedure, find all the places the turtle goes forward a number, say **forward 50**. Change that to say **forward 50 * :size**. Remember that * is computer-ese for multiplication, and **:size** means "what's in size." Use copy and paste to drop the "* :size" into the right places. Don't change the angle inputs, though, where the turtle is turning right or left. Don't change the turtle headings. Now, test your program. Does it resize the house if you ask for a small house?

Oops! We'll need to resize the windows too! We need to draw big windows or small windows, depending on whether the user chose *big* or *small*.

For starters, let's do the same thing as before, and create an input variable for **1window** and **2window**; in other words, from **Main** we'll call these procedures using **1window 1** or **1window 0.5**. Make your changes to the code for **1window** and **2window**—add a variable to the first line of the procedure, such as **w1size** and **w2size**. Inside the procedures, multiply every call to forward by **what's in w1size** or **what's in w2size**, such as :

forward 10 * :w1size

Now, take a look at our **Main** code.

> **question [I will build you a house. Do you want big or small?]**
> **ifelse (answer = "big) [house 1][house 0.5]**

The second line, you recall, means that if the answer is big, call **house** 1; otherwise, call **house** 0.5. OK, that part works great. Here we have input from the user and use it to choose whether to build a big house or a small house. Next:

> **question [Do you want 1 or 2 windows?]**
> **ifelse (answer = 1) [1window][2window]**

Oops, we have a problem! Here, we have more input from the user, this time on the number of windows. We have now lost the input about big or small house—it isn't stored anywhere. So if we want to make a change to draw a big or small window, we don't know which!

Think about how to solve this problem. You're an experienced programmer now, and you should be able to come up with a solution before you turn the page!

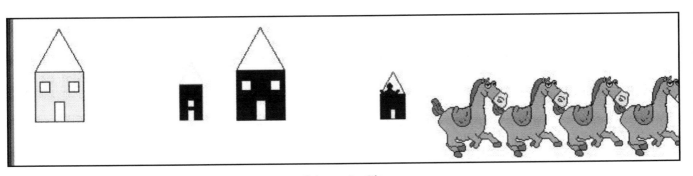

Lianna's City

We need to create a variable to store the size indicated by the user long enough to use it in the calls to **1window** and **2window**. This variable will be *local* to **Main.** (A local variable is one that is not usable in another procedure. One which is usable in all procedures is a *global* variable. This is poor programming practice, with plenty of room for bugs.) Since programmers generally declare all variables at the top of a procedure, insert a first line in **Main** that creates a local variable called **hsize**. Look up the procedure **local** in the Help vocabulary before you do it.

Now, where will you use **hsize**? You need to store the user's preference in it. In the line that says

> **ifelse (answer = "big) [house 1][house 0.5]**

you will need to add to the stuff in the brackets, so that

> **;if the answer is big, call house with input 1 and make what's in hsize 1**
> **;otherwise call house with input 0.5 and make what's in hsize 0.5.**

Can you translate that pseudocode to Logo? Look up **make** in the help vocabulary to make sure you are using it right.

Also use **hsize** to:

- re-size the windows and

- resize the distance in **Main** that moves the turtle down the street before it starts to draw again.

Get this to work by the beginning of the next class.

Crystal's City

#33 City III

Your City project should be working well now, except for the animations. Hatch four more turtles.

Let's write our animation for **t2**. Remember, this is how we set up an animation:

- Talk to that turtle. Show turtle (**st**); set heading (**seth**).

- Make your shapes if you want. Install them if you need to.

- Using setshape, or **setsh,** we give a list of shapes for a turtle to take, one after the other, for example, **setsh [horse1 horse2].**

- Next, we set up a situation that repeatedly calls **forward**. Each time **forward** is called, a new shape is used. For example, **repeat 10 [forward 3].**

- Next, put in a pause to make the action more realistic. Use **wait.** For example, **repeat 10 [forward 3 wait 1].**

Use the shapes in the shape center (be sure to scroll down to see them all), change them, or create your own. To change or create a shape, double click on a shape or on a shape blank, and use the drawing tools. Be sure you give them unique names. You can use two or three as an action sequence. Here's how to copy a shape that exists in order to paste it onto another shape blank and change it slightly: select the shape in the shape center (you see a square around it). Hit **control-c** to copy it to the clipboard. Now select a shape blank. You see a square around it. Hit **control-v** to paste the shape there. Double click on it now to make your changes. You can change the shape's color using the fill bucket or a very fat line. If you are animating a vehicle, make its lights blink or change color as it moves.

Now, to get each animation to work as an independent process, use **launch**. **Launch** works with **repeat**, like this:

> **talkto "t2**
> **launch [repeat 5000 [forward 3 wait 1]]**

One more thing: we need to adjust **setup** to take into account the animating turtles. Add some lines to setup that do this:

> **;talk to t2, t3, t4 and t5,**
> **;pull pen up, hide turtle**
> **;set position at some starting point in your street. All these turtles can start at the same point.**

And, don't forget to show turtle (**st**) in the **animate** procedure.

By the beginning of next class, get the animations to work, and finish the game. Draw a background, such as mountains or trees, using the drawing center tools.

Extra Credit Exercises

1. Add another option to the game. Make two house designs, and ask the user to select one. First ask if the user wants big or small, then ask the user to choose a house design, then number of windows, then color. Note: this is a complicated assignment! It is also our last Logo assignment. Are you up to it?

2. Cause night to fall as your animated characters start going across the screen. This is particularly effective if you have vehicles with blinking lights.

Tiffany's City

Paul's Army Camp, nightfall. Note the two house styles.

Appendix I

MicroWorlds Troubleshooting and Procedure Names

Troubleshooting Guide

Make sure there are spaces between each word and between word and symbol, for example

colorunder = 15

Make sure each procedure starts with **to** and ends with **end**.

Make sure there are brackets [like these] around lists. List items are separated by spaces. For example:

setsh [horse1 horse2 horse3]

In the above example, note that the names **horse1, horse2,** and **horse3** contain no spaces.

For words used as names or nouns (not procedure names, which are actions) make sure there are double-quote marks like these **"word** , made with a single stroke of the double-quote key, or else put the words into a list with brackets. If the error message says "I don't know how to word," then you have forgotten to label **word** as a noun by using either the quote marks or the brackets. So the computer thinks it is an action word. (Or perhaps **word** is a procedure name and you have forgotten to write the procedure for **word**.)

If you can't figure out where the problem is in the program, insert some signal flags. Put lines into the code that say **show "OK** in several places. The program will print **OK** in the Command Center when it passes those spots. Then you will know where to concentrate your efforts, where it is not printing out. Remove these lines when you figure out the problem.

If your program isn't running right, it may be organized poorly. Check the logic of the sequence of things you are calling on the computer to do. If necessary, look at the answers in the answer key.

If you use a built-in procedure name by accident for one of your procedures or variable names, the program won't run right.

If you get an error message about turtles, perhaps you forgot to hatch the turtles called for.

If you use a capital O instead of a zero (0), the program won't run right.

If the error message says a procedure needs more inputs, concentrate on the line that calls that procedure and the one following, and look for the proper number of inputs and the proper number of opening and closing brackets.

If you run through this checklist and it still isn't working, try this: use **Cut** and **Paste** to move your code around on the Procedures Page. This especially works if MicroWorlds is pretending not to see one of your procedures.

Some Built-in Procedures (see Index for more):

cc clear the Command Center.

cg clears graphics.

pd puts the current turtle's pen down and requires no inputs and has no outputs.

forward or **fd** moves the current turtle in the direction its head is pointing by a number of steps. The number of steps is a required input. (**back** does the opposite).

right turns the current turtle to the right by a number of degrees. The number is a required input. (**left** does the opposite.)

wait takes one input, a number.

repeat requires two inputs: a number indicating how many repetitions, and a list of instructions to repeat. A list has brackets [ ] around it.

Presentation Mode: Go to the Gadgets menu and click on Presentation Mode. Then click the Start button. To get out of Presentation Mode, click on the black part of the screen outside of MicroWorlds.

talkto "t1 works with turtle named t1.

setc setcolor, takes a number input, sets the color the turtle is drawing.

random takes a number input, randomly produces a number less than the input.

setc random 100 will generate a random new color every time it is repeated.

fill fills the area the turtle is in with the color the turtle is set to.

seth set heading, sets the direction the turtle will move. Takes a number input. 0 is up, is to the right, -90 or 270 is to the left, 180 is down. Example: **seth 90.**

setsh, set shape, requires an input which is either a word (must be the name of a shape, such as **setsh "horse1**) or a list of words (must be a list of names of shapes). It changes the shape of the turtle. Point to a particular turtle first using **talkto.** If you give a list of shapes, the program will pick a new shape from the list every time it calls **forward** or **back.**

local reserves and names a storage place.

make puts a value in it.

show takes one input, a word or a list, and prints it on the Command Center.

: is read, "the value that is in" the storage place or variable.

ycor has as output the Ycoordinate (height on the screen) of the turtle.

xcor has as output the x coordinate (distance from the left side) of the turtle.

sety takes a number as an input and sets the Ycoordinate.

setx takes a number as input and sets the x coordinate.

launch has as an input a list of instructions [using brackets like this] to run as a separate process.

Appendix II

Part 1 Answers

#2 answers

```
To square
  ;draws a square of 50 units
  pd
  repeat 4 [forward 50 right 90 wait 1]
end
```

#4 answers

```
============

to Main
  cc
  pu
  talkto "t1
  ;works with turtle named t1
  setsh [dog1 dog2] or [doggy1 doggy2]
  seth -90
  repeat 20 [fd 2 wait 2]
end

============

to square
  ;draws a square of 50 units
  pd
  repeat 4 [forward 50 right 90 wait 1]
end

to Start
  Main
end
```

#5 answers

```
to square
  ; draws a square of 50 units
  pd
  forward 50 right 90 wait 1
  forward 50 right 90 wait 1
  forward 50 right 90 wait 1
  forward 50 right 90 wait 1
end
```

becomes

```
to square
  ;draws a square of 50 units
  pd
  repeat 4 [forward 50 right 90 wait 1]
end
```

Drawing a starburst

```
to starburst
  pd
  repeat 360 [right 1 forward 50 back  50]
end
```

Drawing a triangle

```
to triangle
  ; draws a triangle of 3 sides of 50
  pd
  repeat 3 [forward 50 right 120 wait 1]
end
to climb.to.roof
  ; takes turtle to position to draw roof
  pu
  seth 0
  forward 50
  right 30
  pd
end

to Main
  ; draws a simple house
  cg
  pd
  square
  climb.to.roof
  triangle
end
```

#6 answers (procedures in alphabetical order)

```
============

to Main
  ;draws a house
  cg
  pd
  square
```

187

```
    climb.to.roof
    triangle
     move.to.door
     door
    move.to.window
    window
     colorhouse
end
```

```
to climb.to.roof
   ; takes turtle to position to draw roof
   pu
   seth 0
    forward 50
    right 30
    pd
end
```

```
to colorhouse
    pu
    seth -90
    forward 5
    setc 15
    fill
end
```

```
to door
   pd
   repeat 2 [forward 20 right 90 forward 10 right
90  wait 1]
end
```

```
to move.to.door
   pu
    seth 180
     forward 50
   left 90
    forward 20
    seth 0
end
```

```
to move.to.window
   pu
    seth 90
    forward 13
    left 90
    forward 30
end
```

```
to square
   ;draws a square of 50 units
    repeat 4 [forward 50 right 90 wait 1]
end
```

```
to triangle
   ; draws a triangle of 3 sides of 50
    repeat 3 [forward 50 right 120 wait 1]
end
```

```
to window
   pd
   repeat 4 [forward 15 right 90]
end
```

#9 answers

```
to Main
    cc
    testSize
end
```

```
to Start
   Main
end
```

```
to testSize
    local "size
    make "size 5
    local "height
    make "height 60
    show :size
    show :height
    make "size sum :size 3
    show :size
end
```

#10 answers

```
to window :size
    repeat 2 [forward 15 * :size  right 90 forward 20 * :size right 90]
end
```

```
to Main
    ;draws a house
    cg
    pd
    square 0.5
    climb.to.roof  0.5
    triangle 0.5
     door 0.5
end
```

```
to climb.to.roof :height
    ; takes turtle to position to draw roof
    pu
    forward 50 * :height
    right 30
    pd
end
```

```
to door :doorsize
    pu
    seth 180
    pd
    forward 50 * :doorsize
   left 90
    forward 15 * :doorsize
    pd
    repeat 4 [forward 20 * :doorsize left 90 wait 1]
end
```

```
to square :length
   ;draws a square of 50 units
    repeat 4 [forward 50 * :length right 90 wait 1]
end
```

188

```
to triangle :trisize
  ; draws a triangle
  repeat 3 [forward 50 * :trisize right 120 wait 1]
end
```

Extra credit:

```
to Main :housesize
  ;draws a house
  cg
  pd
  square :housesize
  climb.to.roof :housesize
  triangle :housesize
  door :housesize
end
```

#11 suggested answers

Bee with wobble down. For MicroWorlds EX,
install and use bird1 and bird2 instead of bee1
and bee2.

```
to Main
  cg
  cc
  talkto "t1
  setsh [bee1 bee2] or bird1 bird2
  seth 90
  repeat 200 [fly 1 10 wobble 10]
end
```

```
to wobble :howFar
  seth 180
  forward :howFar
  wait 1
  back :howFar
  seth 90
end
```

```
to Start
  Main
end
```

```
to fly :stepsize :qsteps
  repeat :qsteps
  [forward :stepsize wait 1]
end
```

Bee or bird wobbles up and then down

```
to Main
  cg
  cc
  talkto "t1
  setsh [bee1 bee2] or bird1 bird2
  seth 90
  repeat 200 [fly 10 10  upwobble 10 fly 10 10
  d_wobble 10]
```

```
end
```

```
to d_wobble :howFar
  seth 180
  forward :howFar
  wait 1
  back :howFar
  seth 90
end
```

```
to fly :stepsize :qsteps
  repeat :qsteps
  [forward :stepsize wait 1]
end
```

```
to start
  main
end
```

```
to upwobble :howFar
  seth 0
  forward :howFar
  wait 1
  back :howFar
  seth 90
end
```

#12 suggested answers

Exercise 1
Make a "Hop" button.

```
to Main
  cc
  talkto "t1
  setsh [dog1 dog2]
  seth 270
  repeat 200
          [Walk 10 10]
end
```

```
to doHop :width
  local "originalX
  make "originalX xcor
  setx sum xcor :width
  wait 1
  setx :originalX
end
```

```
to doJump :height
  local "originalY
  make "originalY ycor
  sety sum ycor :height
  wait 1
  sety :originalY
end
```

```
to hop
  doHop 45  ;(change this number to several other
;numbers and see the result)
end
```

```
to jump
  doJump 40
```

189

```
end

to Start
   Main
end

to walk :stepsize :qsteps
   repeat :qsteps
      [forward :stepsize  wait 1]
end
```

Exercise 2
Change Main as follows:
```
to Main
   cc cg pu
   talkto "t1
   setsh [horse1 horse2 horse3]
   seth 90
   repeat 200
           [Walk 10 10]
   end
```

Exercise 3
Change Main as follows:
```
   repeat 200
           [Walk 2 8]
```
Exercise 4
Change walk as follows:
```
to walk :stepsize :qsteps
   repeat :qsteps
      [setx sum xcor :stepsize
      wait 1 ]
end
```
(Note: without forward, the animal doesn't
appear to walk any more.)

#13 suggested answers

*ex. 1 & 2   Add two turtles; install tornado1 and
tornado2 shapes, and also lightning2. Give t4 a
castle shape by clicking on it. Program the color
cyan to respond to colorCyanHit. Spray some cyan
paint near the castle.*

```
to Main
   cc cg pu
   talkto "t2
   setsh [dog1 dog2]
   seth 270
   launch
      |
      repeat 200
        [Walk 10 10]
      |
   talkto "t3
   setsh [skater1 skater2 skater3]
   seth 90
   launch
      |
      repeat 200
        [walk 10 10]
      |
   talkto "t5
   setsh [tornado1 tornado2]
   seth 90
   launch
      |
```

```
      repeat 200
           [walk 10 10]
      |
end
```

```
to colorCyanHit
   doJump 80 200
   poof
   wait 5
   unpoof
end
```

```
to colorGrayHit
   doJump 50 100
end
```

```
to doJump :height :distance
   local "originalY
   make "originalY ycor
   sety sum ycor :height
   wait 1
   forward :distance
   wait 1
   sety :originalY
end
```

```
to jump
   doJump 30 30
end
```

```
to poof
   talkto "t4
   setsh "cloud or "lightning2
end
```

```
to Start
   Main
end
```

```
to unpoof
   talkto "t4
   setsh "castle
end
```

```
to walk :stepsize :qsteps
   repeat :qsteps
      [forward :stepsize
      wait 1]
end
```

190

ex. 3

Draw a spiral maze using the drawing center and a thick gray line. Program the color gray to respond to colorGrayHit.

Here is one possibility for a maze, not the best—can you do a better one?

```
to Main
  cc
  talkto "t1
  setsh 0
  repeat 2000 [ forward 1 ]
end

to colorGrayHit
  back 3 wait 1
  right random 270
  wait 1
  forward 3 wait 1
end

to Start
  Main
end
```

Appendix III

Part 2 Answers

#15 MADLIBS SOLUTIONS

All the print-sentence possibilities will work. Be sure you first make a text box on Page1.

PSEUDOCODE:

```
to madlibs
;Create and name variables
;Ask the user to type in an animal name.
;Store the animal name in a variable named noun1.
;Ask the user for the name of an object.
;Store this as noun2.
;Ask the user to name something he or she likes to do.
;Store this as noun3.
;Ask the user to describe a feeling.
;Store this as adj1.
;Ask for an adverb, such as slowly, quickly, heavily, etc.
;Store this as adv1.
;Announce that here is the Madlib.
;print  "There once was a "noun1. One day the noun1 went to
the park and saw a ;noun2.  The noun1 adv1 ate the noun2 and
then went for a noun3.  After that the ;noun1 was feeling a
little adj1.  Adv1 the noun1 went home and took a nap."
end
```

CODE:

```
to madlibs
  local [noun1 noun2 noun3 noun4 adj1 adv1]
  question [Please type in an animal name.]
  make "noun1 answer
  question [Please type in the name of an object.]
  make "noun2 answer
 question [Please type in the name of something you like to do.]
  make "noun3 answer
  question [Please describe a feeling.]
  make "adj1 answer
 question [Give me an adverb, such as slowly, quickly, heavily,
etc.]
  make "adv1 answer
  announce [Here is your madlib.]
  print (sentence [There once was a | :noun1 )
  print (sentence [.  One day the | :noun1 )
  print (sentence [went to the park and saw a | :noun2 [.])
  print (sentence [The] :noun1 [ate the | :noun2 [and then ])
  print (sentence [went for a | :noun3 [.])
  print (sentence [After that the | :noun1 [was feeling a little |
:adj1 [.])
  print (sentence [Then] :adv1 [the] :noun1)
  print (sentence  [went home and took a nap.])
end
```

Now, be sure you add the Main and the Start button to get a complete program:

```
to Main
  madlibs
```

```
end

to Start
  Main
end
```

#16 MADLIBS II SOLUTIONS

```
to Main
  intro
end
```

```
to intro
  question [What's your name?]; makes a dialogue box
  announce [I like your name.] ; dialogue box without space
  question [Would you like to play Madlibs? Y or N]
  if (answer = "Y) [madlibs]
  announce "Bye!
end
```

```
to madlibs
  local [noun1 noun2 noun3 noun4 adj1 adv1]
  question [Please type in an animal name.]
  make "noun1 answer
  question [Please type in the name of an object.]
  make "noun2 answer
 question [Please type in the name of something you like to do.]
  make "noun3 answer
  question [Please describe a feeling.]
  make "adj1 answer
question [Give me an adverb, such as slowly, quickly, heavily, etc.]
  make "adv1 answer
  announce [Here is your madlib.]
  print (sentence [There once was a | :noun1 )
  print (sentence [.  One day the | :noun1 )
  print (sentence [went to the park and saw a | :noun2 [.])
  print (sentence [The] :noun1 [ate the | :noun2 [and then ])
  print (sentence [went for a | :noun3 [.])
  print (sentence [After that the | :noun1 [was feeling a little |
:adj1 [.])
  print (sentence [Then] :adv1 [the] :noun1)
  print (sentence  [went home and sat on the roof.])
end
```

```
to Start
  Main
end
```

FOR EXERCISE 1:

```
to intro
  question [What's your name?]; makes a dialogue box
  announce [I like your name.] ; dialogue box without space
  question [Would you like to play Madlibs? Y or N]
  ifelse  (answer = "Y) [madlibs] [announce "Bye!]
end
```

FOR EXERCISE 2, ONE QUESTION GUESSING GAME:

```
to Main
  oneq
end
```

```
to intro
  question [What's your name?]; makes a dialogue box
  announce [I like your name.] ; dialogue box without space
  question [Would you like to play One Question? Y or N]
  ifelse (answer = "y) [oneq]  [announce [Bye!]]
end
```

```
to oneq
  local "quiznumber
  make "quiznumber 4
  question [Guess a number between 0 and 10.]
  if (answer > :quiznumber) [announce  [Too big!]]
  if (answer < :quiznumber) [announce [Too small!]]
  if (answer = :quiznumber) [announce  [You got it!]]
  print (sentence [The number was] :quiznumber)
end
```

```
to Start
  Main
end
```

#17 ANIMATION USING VARIABLES SOLUTIONS

EXERCISE 2, GUESSING GAME WITH JIG ADDED:

```
to Main
  intro
end
```

```
to intro
  question [What's your name?]; makes a dialogue box
  announce [I like your name.] ; dialogue box without space
  question [Would you like to play One Question? Y or N]
  ifelse (answer = "Y) [oneq]
  [announce [Bye!]]
end
```

```
to jig
announce [You got it!]
talkto "t1
pd
repeat 30 [fd 2 wait 1 right 10 fd 4 wait 1 left 25]
end
```

```
to oneq
  local "quiznumber
  make "quiznumber 4
  question [Guess a number between 0 and 10.]
```

```
  if (answer > :quiznumber) [announce  [Too big!]]
  if (answer < :quiznumber) [announce [Too small!]]
  if (answer = :quiznumber) [jig]
  print (sentence [The number was] :quiznumber)
end
```

```
to Start
  Main
end
```

#18 WANDERING TURTLE SOLUTIONS

```
to Main
  repeat 60
    [wander 5]
end
```

```
to wander :stepSize
  pd
  ; turn right by a random amount which could be negative
  right  difference random 100 50
  ; move forward by stepSize, repeat twice
  repeat 2 [forward :stepSize wait 1]
end
```

```
to Start
  Main
end
```

#18 EXERCISES

1. *Adjust the stepSize.* Change wander 5 to wander 9 or whatever.
2. *Adjust the input to make smoother lines. How do you do that?*
   Change the input to **random.** *How do you need to adjust the number subtracted from the random number?* Make it half the input to random. For example, **difference random 100 50** can become **difference random 40 20.**
3. *Make the turtle's shape change as it wanders around. Hint: use* **setsh** *in* **Main.** *See below.*

```
to Main
  setsh [horse1 horse2 horse3]
  repeat 60  [wander 5]
end
```

```
to Start
  Main
end
```

```
to wander :stepSize
  pd
  ; turn right by a random amount which could be negative
  right difference random 100 50
  ; move forward by stepSize, repeat twice
  repeat 2 [forward :stepSize wait 1]
end
```

#19 ENHANCED WANDERING TURTLE SOLUTIONS

EXERCISE 5

```
to wander :stepSize :dizziness
   pd
   ; turn right by a random amount which could be negative
   ; turn right by a random amount up to dizziness
   right difference random :dizziness  quotient :dizziness 2
   ; move forward by stepSize, repeat twice
   repeat 2 [forward :stepSize wait 1]
end
```

#21 MAZE II: WIN OR LOSE?

A basic maze:

Create a button labeled "go." Draw a maze using thick red lines from the Drawing Center (under the paintbrush icon). Be sure the color you are using is labeled 15; pause your mouse over the color in the Drawing Center to be sure.

```
to Main
   talkto "t1
   launch [repeat 2000 [forward 3 direct readchar ] ]
   waituntil [colorunder = 15]
   announce [You lose!]
   reset
end
```

```
to direct :key
   if (ascii :key) = 28 [seth 270 fd 1]
   if (ascii :key) = 29 [seth 90 fd 1]
   if (ascii :key) = 30 [seth 0 fd 1]
   if (ascii :key) = 31 [seth 180 fd 1]
   if (ascii :key) = 37 [seth 270 fd 1]
   if (ascii :key) = 39 [seth 90 fd 1]
   if (ascii :key) = 38 [seth 0 fd 1]
   if (ascii :key) = 40 [seth 180 fd 1]
   if (:key = "s) [stopall]
end
```

```
to go
   Main
end
```

```
to reset
   talkto "t1
   setpos [-319 -164]
   seth 0
end
```

EXERCISES:

1. Use the turtle-hatching button to place a new turtle at the destination point in the maze. This is **t2**.
2. Add underlined line, and add a shape **dog1** to your Shape Center if you have MicroWorlds EX.

```
to Main
   talkto "t1
   setsh 0
   launch [repeat 2000 [forward 3 direct readchar ] ]
   when [touching? "t1 "t2] [setsh "dog1 ]
   waituntil [colorunder = 15]
   announce [You lose!]
   reset
end
```

Flow chart addition:

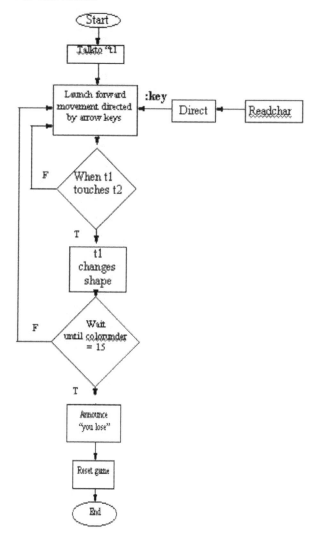

3. In MicroWorlds EX, you will need to install a castle and a cloud into your Shape Center from the Drawing Center list of single shapes (in the Pinting/Clipart window under the flower icon). Click on the castle and then on T2 to change its shape to a castle.

Turtle 1 changes to random shapes when it hits the castle:

Add some shapes to the first 9 blanks in your Shapes Center. This is so we can change shapes using **random 10**, and get a random choice of those 9 shapes.

```
to Main
    talkto "t1
    launch [repeat 2000 [forward 3 direct readchar ] ]
    when [touching? "t1 "t2] [win]
    waituntil [colorunder = 15]
    announce [You lose!]
    reset
end
```

```
to direct :key
    if (ascii :key) = 28 [seth 270 fd 1]
    if (ascii :key) = 29 [seth 90 fd 1]
    if (ascii :key) = 30 [seth 0 fd 1]
    if (ascii :key) = 31 [seth 180 fd 1]
    if (ascii :key) = 37 [seth 270 fd 1]
    if (ascii :key) = 39 [seth 90 fd 1]
    if (ascii :key) = 38 [seth 0 fd 1]
    if (ascii :key) = 40 [seth 180 fd 1]
    if (:key = "s) [stopall]
end
to go
    Main
end
```

```
to win
    announce [You win!]
    talkto "t1
    setsh "cloud wait 2
    setsh random 10 wait 10
end
```

```
to reset
    talkto "t1
    setpos [-319 -164]
end
```

4. Change **win** to this, adding underlined line:

```
to win
    announce [You win!]
    talkto "t1
    setsh "cloud wait 2
    setsh random 10 wait 10
    reset
end
```

Change reset to this, adding underlined line:

```
to reset
    talkto "t1
    setpos [-319 -164]
    seth 0
    setsh 0
end
```

5. Add flow chart to describe what we have so far:

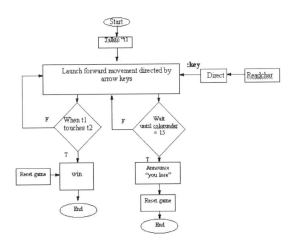

PRINCE/PRINCESS PROJECT: Game asks the user whether the user would rather be a prince or a princess, and the turtle turns into a boy or girl when it gets to the castle. If you have MicroWorlds EX, load a boy shape into blank number 41, and a girl shape into blank number 40. If you have MicroWorlds 2.0, use **cloud** instead of **lightning1**.

```
to Main
    local "preference
    announce [Hi!  If you get to the castle, you will be changed
back  into a human.]
    question [Would you like to be a prince or a princess? B for
boy or G for girl]
    ifelse (answer = "B) [make "preference 41] [make
"preference 40]
    talkto "t1
    launch [repeat 2000 [forward 3 direct readchar ] ]
    when [touching? "t1 "t2] [win "preference]
    waituntil [colorunder = 15]
    announce [You lose!]
    reset
end
```

```
to direct :key
    if (ascii :key) = 28 [seth 270 fd 1]
    if (ascii :key) = 29 [seth 90 fd 1]
    if (ascii :key) = 30 [seth 0 fd 1]
    if (ascii :key) = 31 [seth 180 fd 1]
    if (ascii :key) = 37 [seth 270 fd 1]
    if (ascii :key) = 39 [seth 90 fd 1]
    if (ascii :key) = 38 [seth 0 fd 1]
    if (ascii :key) = 40 [seth 180 fd 1]
    if (:key = "s) [stopall]
end
```

```
to win :gender
  announce [You win!]
  talkto "t1
  setsh "lightning1 wait 2
  setsh :gender wait 10
  reset
end
to go
  Main
end

to reset
  talkto "t1
  setpos [-319 -164]
  seth 0
  setsh 0
end
```

#22 MAZE III

```
to Main
  talkto "t1
  launch [repeat 2000 [forward 3 direct readchar ] ]
  talkto "t3
  launch [repeat 2000 [forward 3 wait 3]]
  when [colorunder = 15] [right 190]
  talkto "t4
  launch [repeat 2000 [forward 3 wait 3]]
  when [colorunder = 15] [right 190]
  talkto "t1
  when [colorunder = 15] [lose]
  when [touching? "t1 "t2] [win]
  when [touching? "t1 "t3] [lose]
  when [touching? "t1 "t4] [lose]
end

to direct :key
  if (ascii :key) = 28 [seth 270 fd 1]
  if (ascii :key) = 29 [seth 90 fd 1]
  if (ascii :key) = 30 [seth 0 fd 1]
  if (ascii :key) = 31 [seth 180 fd 1]
  if (ascii :key) = 37 [seth 270 fd 1]
  if (ascii :key) = 39 [seth 90 fd 1]
  if (ascii :key) = 38 [seth 0 fd 1]
  if (ascii :key) = 40 [seth 180 fd 1]
  if (:key = "s) [stopall]
end

to go
  Main
end

to win
  announce [You win!]
  talkto "t1
  setsh "cloud wait 2
  setsh random 60 wait 10
  reset
end
```

```
to reset
  talkto "t1
  setpos [-319 -164]
  seth 0
  setsh 0
end
to lose
  announce [You lose!]
  wait 5
  reset
end
```

#23 MAZE IV

```
to Maineasy
  talkto "t1
  launch [repeat 2000 [forward 3 direct readchar ] ]
  talkto "t3
  launch [repeat 2000 [forward 3 wait 3]]
  when [colorunder = 15] [right 190]
  talkto "t4
  launch [repeat 2000 [forward 3 wait 3]]
  when [colorunder = 15] [right 190]
  talkto "t1
  when [colorunder = 15] [lose]
  when [touching? "t1 "t2] [win]
  when [touching? "t1 "t3] [lose]
  when [touching? "t1 "t4] [lose]
end

to Mainmedium
  talkto "t1
  launch [repeat 2000 [forward 3 direct readchar ] ]
  talkto "t3
  launch [repeat 2000 [forward 3 wait 2]]
  when [colorunder = 15] [right 190]
  talkto "t4
  launch [repeat 2000 [forward 3 wait 2]]
  when [colorunder = 15] [right 190]
  talkto "t1
  when [colorunder = 15] [lose]
  when [touching? "t1 "t2] [win]
  when [touching? "t1 "t3] [lose]
  when [touching? "t1 "t4] [lose]
end

to Mainhard
  talkto "t1
  launch [repeat 2000 [forward 3 direct readchar ] ]
  talkto "t3
  launch [repeat 2000 [forward 4 wait 2]]
  when [colorunder = 15] [right 190]
  talkto "t4
  launch [repeat 2000 [forward 4 wait 2]]
  when [colorunder = 15] [right 190]
  talkto "t1
  when [colorunder = 15] [lose]
  when [touching? "t1 "t2] [win]
  when [touching? "t1 "t3] [lose]
```

```
when [touching? "t1 "t4] [lose]
end
```

```
to direct :key
  if (ascii :key) = 28 [seth 270 fd 1]
  if (ascii :key) = 29 [seth 90 fd 1]
  if (ascii :key) = 30 [seth 0 fd 1]
  if (ascii :key) = 31 [seth 180 fd 1]
  if (ascii :key) = 37 [seth 270 fd 1]
  if (ascii :key) = 39 [seth 90 fd 1]
  if (ascii :key) = 38 [seth 0 fd 1]
  if (ascii :key) = 40 [seth 180 fd 1]
  if (:key = "s) [stopall]
end

to easy
  easypage
  Maineasy
end

to hard
  hardpage
  Mainhard
end

to index
  Page1
end

to lose
  announce [You lose!]
  wait 5
  reset
end

to medium
  mediumpage
  Mainmedium
end

to reset
  talkto "t1
  setpos [-319 -164]
  seth 0
  setsh 0
end

to win
  announce [You win!]
  talkto "t1
  setsh "cloud wait 2
  setsh random 60 wait 10
  reset
end
```

EXERCISES

---

*1. Add teleporter booths. Here's how: put a box of another color into the maze. When the **t1** turtle hits the color, it jumps to a different spot in the maze. To find the coordinates of the spot you want to teleport to, move the turtle there using the mouse, and then type **show pos** in the Command Center.*

Make a sky blue box (color is 95) somewhere in your medium maze. **Mainmedium** will contain this section, with new line underlined:

```
talkto "t1
when [colorunder = 15] [lose]
when [colorunder =  95] [setpos 18 –146]
when [touching? "t1 "t2] [win]
```

*2. Create animations using a list of shapes with **setsh** and repeated calls to **forward**.*

Have the t1 turtle animate when it reaches the goal. Make sure there are shapes in your Shape Center to use. Add underlined lines:

```
to win
  announce [You win!]
  talkto "t1
  setsh "cloud wait 2
  setsh random 60 wait 10
  setsh [horse1 horse2 horse3]
  seth 90
  repeat 10 [forward 1 wait 1]
  reset
end
```

Make an animation for the spiders (t3 and t4) as they move, giving realistic motion. Make sure there are shapes in your Shape Center to use. I will use bird1 and bird2 for MicroWorlds EX, and bee1 and bee2 for MicroWorlds 2.0. Add underlined lines:

```
to Maineasy
  talkto "t1
  launch [repeat 2000 [forward 3 direct readchar] ]
  talkto "t3
  setsh [bird1 bird2]
  launch [repeat 2000 [forward 3 wait 3]]
  when [colorunder = 15] [right 190]
  talkto "t4
  setsh [bird1 bird2]
  launch [repeat 2000 [forward 3 wait 3]]
  when [colorunder = 15] [right 190]
  ...
```

Animate the t1 turtle as it goes through the maze. One possibility: make it look like Pac-Man, an ancient videogame hero who looks like a yellow cookie. You can make new shapes by double-clicking on the blank shapes in the shape center, and using drawing tools to construct them. Construct shapes and call them pac1, pac2, and pac3, for example. Then add underlined line:

```
to Maineasy
  talkto "t1
  setsh [pac1 pac2 pac3 pac2]
  launch [repeat 2000 [forward 3 direct readchar] ]
  ...
```

197

#24 RACE I

Save your sketch to compare to the flow chart in the next lesson.

#25 RACE II

Note: You may need to thicken your finish line. Identify its color number as you draw it. In MicroWorlds EX, Import shapes to use for your winning animation, such as bird1 and bird2, or in MicroWorlds 2.0 use bee1 and bee2.
==============

```
to Main
 setup
 question [Player 1, What is the height of Mount Everest in miles?]
 ifelse (answer = "6)
        [talkto "t1 fd 170][announce [Wrong answer!  It was 6.]]
 wait 5
 question [Player 2, What is the depth of the Marianas Trench in miles?]
 ifelse (answer = "6)
        [talkto "t2 fd 170] [announce [Wrong answer!  It was 6.]]
 wait 5
 question [Player 1, What is the mountain range of Mt. Everest?]
 ifelse (answer = "Himalayas )
        [talkto "t1 fd 170] [announce [Wrong answer! It was Himalayas.]
 wait 5
 question [Player 2, What is the word for a monk in Tibet?]
 ifelse (answer = "Lama)
         [talkto "t2 fd 170] [announce [Wrong answer! It was Lama.]]
 wait 5
 question [Player 1,What man from India inspired Martin Luther King
Jr.?]
 ifelse (answer = "Gandhi)
        [talkto "t1 fd 170] [announce [Wrong answer!  It was Gandhi.]]
 wait 5
 question [Player 2, What is the main religion in India?]
 ifelse (answer = "Hinduism)
        [talkto "t2 fd 170] [announce [Wrong answer!  It was Hinduism.]]
 wait 5
 question [Player 1, What is the main religion in Pakistan and
Bangladesh?]
 ifelse (answer = "Islam)
        [talkto "t1 fd 170][announce [Wrong answer!  It was Islam.]]
 wait 5
 question [Player 2, in what country is Mount Everest?]
 ifelse (answer = "Nepal)
        [talkto "t2 fd 170][announce [Wrong answer! It was Nepal.]]
 wait 5
 talkto [t1 t2]
 if (colorunder = 15)[ win]
end
```
==============
```
    to win
     talkto "t3
     st; shows turtle
     setsh [bird1 bird2]
     repeat 30 [forward .01 wait 2]
    end

    to setup
     talkto "t1
```

```
setpos [-346 -73]
seth 90
talkto "t2
setpos [-346 -151]
seth 90
talkto "t3
ht ;hides turtle
setpos [340 -117]
seth 90
end


to Start
  Main
end
```

EXERCISE:
Change this line at the end of **Main**:
```
    ifelse (colorunder = 15)[ win] [announce [No winners!]]
    end
```


#26 RACE III

Create a Page2. Create shapes named ball1, fire1, fire2, and fire3. On Page2, make sure there are nine turtles.

Change this procedure:
```
   to win
     Page2
     announce[You win!!!!!]
     talkto [t1 t2 t3 t4 t5 t6 t7 t8 t9]
     setsh [ball1 fire1 fire2 fire3]
      repeat 30 [forward .01 wait 2]
   end
```
Change this procedure:
```
   to setup
    Page1
    talkto "t1
    setpos [-346 -73]
    seth 90
    talkto "t2
    setpos [-346 -151]
    seth 90
    talkto "t3
    ht ;hides turtle
    setpos [340 -117]
    seth 90
   end
```

#27 HANGMAN I: GOING LOOPY

EXERCISE 1: Be sure you have a stopall button and a Start button.
==============
```
to Main
  pd
  forever
  [
    talkto "t1
    seth 0 forward 40 wait 1
    right 170 forward 40 wait 1
```

198

```
    ]
  end
```

```
  to Start
    Main
  end
```

EXERCISE 2
```
    to Main
      local "counter
      make "counter 0
      pd
      forever
      [
        talkto "t1
        seth 0 forward 40 wait 1
        right 170 forward 40 wait 1
        show :counter
        make "counter sum :counter 1
      ]
    end
```

EXERCISE 3 Hatch two more turtles. Install a left-facing set of animations into your Shape Center, and also a right-facing set, if you have MicroWorlds EX. Otherwise just use snake and bee.

```
    to Main
      local "counter
      make "counter 0
      pd
      forever
      [
        talkto "t1
        seth 0 forward 40 wait 1
        right 170 forward 40 wait 1
        show :counter
        make "counter sum :counter 1
        if (:counter = 10) [talkto "t2 seth -90 setsh [bird1 bird2]
repeat 3 [forward 3 wait 1]]
        if (:counter = 20) [talkto "t3 seth 90 setsh [dolphin4
dolphin5 dolphin6] repeat 3 [forward 3 wait 1]]
        if (:counter = 30) [stopall]
      ]
    end
```

```
    to Start
      Main
    end
```

EXERCISE 4
Replace the three **if** statements with these:

```
      when [:counter = 10] [talkto "t2 seth -90 setsh [bird1 bird2]
              repeat 3 [forward 3 wait 1]]
      when [:counter = 20] [talkto "t3 seth 90 setsh [dolphin4 dolphin5
dolphin6]
              repeat 3 [forward 3 wait 1]]
      when [:counter = 30] [stopall]
```

This doesn't work because we can't have lots of processes running at the same time working on the same set of numbers (the counters).

```
    to Main
      local "counter
      make "counter 0

      forever
      [
        question [Please give me a letter]
        if (answer = "d) [talkto "text1 print answer]
        if (answer = "o) [talkto "text2 print answer]
        if (answer = "g) [talkto "text3 print answer]
        show :counter
        if not ( or answer = "d answer = "o answer = "g)
          [make "counter sum :counter 1]
        if (:counter = 6)[stopall]
      ]
    end
```

```
    to Start
      Main
    end
```

Exercises
1: F
2: T
3: T
4: F

#29 HANGMAN III

EXERCISE 1
```
    to Main
      local [counter letter1 letter2 letter3]
      reset
      make "counter 0
      forever
      [
        question [Please give me a letter]
        if (answer = "d) [talkto "text1 print answer make "letter1
answer]
        if (answer = "o) [talkto "text2 print answer make "letter2
answer]
        if (answer = "g) [talkto "text3 print answer make "letter3
answer]
        show :counter
if not ( or answer = "d answer = "o answer = "g) [make
"counter sum :counter 1]
        if (:counter = 6)[announce [You lose!] stopall]
        if (and :letter1 = "d :letter2 = "o :letter3 = "g)[announce
[You win!] stopall]
      ]
    end
```

```
    to reset
```

```
talkto "text1
cleartext
talkto "text2
cleartext
talkto "text3
cleartext
end


to Start
  Main
end
```

#30 HANGMAN IV

```
to Main
  local [counter letter1 letter2 letter3]
  talkto [t1 t2 t3 t4 t5 t6]
  ht
  reset
  make "counter 0
  forever
  [
   question [Please give me a letter]
  if (answer = "d) [talkto "text1 print answer make "letter1
answer]
   if (answer = "o) [talkto "text2 print answer make "letter2
answer]
   if (answer = "g) [talkto "text3 print answer make "letter3
answer]
   show :counter
   if not ( or answer = "d answer = "o answer = "g)
        [make "counter sum :counter 1]
   if (:counter = 1) [talkto "t2 st setsh "noose]
  if (:counter = 2) [talkto "t1 st setsh "head]
  if (:counter = 3) [talkto "t3 st setsh "body]
  if (:counter = 4) [talkto "t5 st setsh "arm2]
  if (:counter = 5) [talkto "t4 st setsh "arm1]
  if (:counter = 6) [talkto "t6 st setsh "legs]
  if (:counter = 6)[announce [You lose!] stopall]
  if (and :letter1 = "d :letter2 = "o :letter3 = "g)
        [announce [You win!] stopall]
  ]
end
```

```
to Start
  Main
end


to reset
  talkto "text1
  cleartext
  talkto "text2
  cleartext
  talkto "text3
  cleartext
end
```

EXERCISE 1: Change underlined lines.

```
to Main
  local [counter letter1 letter2 letter3]
  talkto [t1 t2 t3 t4 t5 t6]
  ht
  reset
  make "counter 0
  forever
  [
   question [Please give me a letter]
   if (answer = "d)
        [talkto "text1 print answer make "letter1 answer]
   if (answer = "o)
        [talkto "text2 print answer make "letter2 answer]
   if (answer = "g)
        [talkto "text3 print answer make "letter3 answer]
   show :counter
   if not ( or answer = "d answer = "o answer = "g)
        [make "counter sum :counter 1]
   if (:counter = 1) [talkto "t2 st setsh "noose]
   if (:counter = 2) [talkto "t1 st setsh "head]
   if (:counter = 3) [talkto "t3 st setsh "body]
   if (:counter = 4) [talkto "t5 st setsh "arm2]
   if (:counter = 5) [talkto "t4 st setsh "arm1]
   if (:counter = 6) [talkto "t6 st setsh "legs]
   if (:counter = 6)
        [announce [You lose!] talkto "t1 st setsh "deadguy
        stopall]
   if (and :letter1 = "d :letter2 = "o :letter3 = "g)
        [announce [You win!] stopall]
  ]
end
```

EXERCISE 2: Change this line near the end of Main, adding "win":

```
   if (and :letter1 = "d :letter2 = "o :letter3 = "g)
        [announce [You win!] win stopall]
```

Add this procedure:

```
to win
  talkto [t2 t3 t4 t5 t6]
  ht
  talkto "t1
  setsh [fire1 fire2]
  repeat 30 [forward 0.01 wait 1]
end
```

#31 CITY I

```
to Main
  talkto "t1
  st
  question [I will build you a house.  Do you want big or
small?]
  ifelse (answer = "big) [house 1][house 0.5]
  wait 5
  question [Do  you want 1 or 2 windows?]
  ifelse (answer = 1) [1window][2window]
```

200

```
    wait 5
    question [Do you want red or blue?]
    ifelse (answer = "red)[fillred][fillblue]
    pu sety -125 seth 90 forward 125 ;move down the street a
ways
    question [Do you want to draw another house? Y or N]
    ifelse (answer = "Y)[Main][animate]
end
```

```
to start
  cg
  setup
  Main
end
```

```
to house :size  ;this procedure doesn't actually use the variable
yet
  seth 0
  pd repeat 4[forward 50 right 90] ;a square
  pu seth 0 forward 50 right 30 pd ;move to roof
  repeat 3[forward 50 right 120 wait 1] ;triangle
  pu seth 180 forward 50 left 90 forward 20 seth 0 ;move to
door
 pd repeat 2 [forward 20 right 90 forward 10 right 90 wait 1]
;door
  pu seth 90 forward 13 left 90 forward 30  ;move to window
end
```

```
to 1window
  pd repeat 4[forward 15 right 90]
end
```

```
to 2window
  pd repeat 4[forward 15 right 90]
  pu seth -90 forward 25 seth 0
  pd repeat 4[forward 15 right 90]
end
```

```
to fillred
  setc 15
  pu seth -100 forward 3 pd
  fill
end
```

```
to fillblue
  setc 105
  pu seth -100 forward 3 pd
  fill
end
```

```
to setup
  talkto "t1
  pu ;pen up
  setpos [-359 -125]
 end
```

```
to animate
end
```

EXERCISE: Here is a preliminary version that uses **forever** to make
the loop. It also doesn't animate or re-size the house yet:

```
to Main
  forever
  [
  talkto "t1
  st
  question [I will build you a house.  Do you want big or
small?]
    ifelse (answer = "big) [house 1][house 0.5]
    wait 5
    question [Do  you want 1 or 2 windows?]
    ifelse (answer = 1) [1window][2window]
    wait 5
    question [Do you want red or blue?]
    ifelse (answer = "red)[fillred][fillblue]
    pu sety -125 seth 90 forward 125 ;move down the street a
ways
    question [Do you want to draw another house? Y or N]
    if (answer = "N)[animate]
    ]
end
```

All other procedures are the same except for this one:

```
to animate
  stopall
end
```

#32 CITY II

```
to Main
  local "hsize
  talkto "t1
  st
  question [I will build you a house.  Do you want big or
small?]
    ifelse (answer = "big) [house 1 make "hsize 1]
      [house 0.5 make "hsize 0.5]
    wait 5
    question [Do  you want 1 or 2 windows?]
    ifelse (answer = 1) [1window :hsize][2window :hsize]
    wait 5
    question [Do you want red or blue?]
    ifelse (answer = "red)[fillred][fillblue]
    pu sety -125 seth 90 forward 125 * :hsize ;move down the
street
    question [Do you want to draw another house? Y or N]
    ifelse (answer = "Y)[Main][animate]
end
```

```
to start
  cg
  setup
  Main
end
```

```
to house :size
```

```
seth 0
pd repeat 4[forward 50 * :size right 90] ;a square
pu seth 0 forward 50 * :size right 30 pd ;move to roof
repeat 3[forward 50 * :size right 120 wait 1] ;triangle
pu seth 180 forward 50 * :size left 90 forward 20 * :size seth 0
;move to door
pd repeat 2 [forward 20 * :size right 90 forward 10 * :size
right 90 wait 1]  ;door
pu seth 90 forward 13 * :size left 90 forward 30 * :size
;move to window
end

to 1window :w1size
pd repeat 4[forward 15 * :w1size right 90]
end

to 2window :w2size
pd repeat 4[forward 15 * :w2size right 90]
pu seth -90 forward 25 * :w2size seth 0
pd repeat 4[forward 15 * :w2size right 90]
end

to fillred
setc 15
pu seth -100 forward 3 pd
fill
end

to fillblue
setc 105
pu seth -100 forward 3 pd
fill
end

to setup
talkto "t1
pu  ;pen up
setpos [-359 -125]
end
```

```
to animate
end
```

#33 CITY III

Make these changes to **setup** and **animate:**

```
to setup
talkto "t1
pu  ;pen up
setpos [-359 -125]
talkto [t2 t3 t4 t5]
pu ht ;pen up, hide turtle
setpos [-359 -130]
end
```

```
to animate
talkto "t2
st seth 90 ;show turtle, set heading to face right
setsh [walker1 walker2 walker3]
launch [repeat 5000 [forward 2 wait 1]]
talkto "t3
st seth 90
setsh [jeep1 jeep2]
launch [repeat 5000 [forward 3 wait 1]]
talkto "t4
st seth 90
setsh [horse1 horse2 horse3]
launch [repeat 5000 [forward 5 wait 1]]
talkto "t5
st seth 90
setsh [skater1 skater2 skater3]
launch [repeat 5000 [forward 3 wait 2]]
end
```

INDEX

Motherboard
Books

www.MotherboardBooks.com